MOTHERS
OF THE
BIBLE

D1173350

Dena Dyer

BARBOUR
PUBLISHING

Published by Barbour Publishing, Inc., P.O. Box 719, Uhrichsville, Ohio 44683, www.barbourbooks.com

Our mission is to publish and distribute inspirational products offering exceptional value and biblical encouragement to the masses.

Printed in the United States of America.

Table of Contents

Introduction

Today's moms feel pressure to guide our children physically, intellectually, emotionally, and spiritually. Those are noble goals for parenting, but the problem is, we never feel that we're doing it right. We're bombarded with advice and parenting tips through television shows, books, Web sites, fellow moms, and grandparents. Each "expert" says their way is the right way. It's enough to make a mom want to run screaming out the door.

Every mom has been there, but guess what? There is a right way to parent—God's way. He tells us everything we need to know in the Bible.

And you know what else? Moms in the scriptures dealt with the same issues moms face today. Rachel, Hannah, and Sarah struggled with infertility. Eunice was a single mom. Eve lost a child, and Naomi lost a spouse. Jochebed gave up her child, and Pharoah's daughter adopted him. Hagar felt rejected, Leah felt unloved, and Job's wife felt abandoned by God.

As you read about these biblical moms, you'll see how God desires to love, guide, and comfort us as parents. Just as in biblical times, He wants to meet us in the midst of our circumstances and prove that we don't have to do the "mom" thing alone. As we read and meditate on the Word of God, He promises to give us the wisdom, patience, and peace we need.

Messy Spirituality
Bathsheba (Part 1)
Abridged from 2 Samuel 11–12 NLV

The spring of the year was the time when kings went out to battle. At that time David sent Joab and his servants and all Israel. . . . But David stayed at Jerusalem.

When evening came, David got up from his bed and walked around on the roof of the king's house. From the roof he saw a woman washing herself. The woman was very beautiful. So David sent someone to ask about the woman. And one said, "Is this not Eliam's daughter Bathsheba, the wife of Uriah the Hittite?" David sent men and took her. When she came to him, he lay with her. After she had made herself clean again, she returned to her house. She was going to have a baby, so she sent someone to tell David, "I am going to have a baby. . . ."

In the morning, David wrote a letter to Joab, and sent it by Uriah. He had written in the letter, "Put Uriah in the front of the hardest battle and come away from him, so that he may be killed."

So while Joab was watching the city, he sent Uriah to the place where he knew there were soldiers with strength of heart. The men of the city went out and fought against Joab. Some of David's servants were killed. And Uriah the Hittite died also. . . .

When Uriah's wife heard that her husband was dead, she was filled with sorrow for him. When the time of sorrow was finished, David sent men and brought her to his house. She became his wife, and gave birth to his son. But what David had done was sinful in the eyes of the Lord.

Then the Lord sent Nathan to David. . . . David said to Nathan, "I have sinned against the Lord." And Nathan said to him, "The Lord has taken away your sin. You will not die. But by this act you have given those who hate the Lord a reason to speak against the Lord. The child that is born to you will die for sure." Then Nathan went home.

The Lord sent trouble upon the child of Uriah's wife and David, so that he was very sick. David begged God to make the child well. He went without food and lay all night on the ground. The leaders of his family stood beside him to lift him up from the ground. But David was not willing. He would not eat food with them. The child died on the seventh day. . . . When David saw his servants speaking together in secret, he understood that the child was dead. He asked his servants, "Is the child dead?" And they said, "He is dead."

So David got up from the ground, washed, poured oil on himself, and changed his clothes. Then he came into the house of the Lord and worshiped. He returned to his own house and asked for food. So they set food in front of him, and he ate. . . .

Then David comforted his wife Bathsheba.

Messy Spirituality
Bathsheba (Part 1)
Life Application

Bathsheba knew the costs, and she must have weighed them. On one hand, she could sleep with the king, even though it was immoral. Her husband was away from home and probably would never know. And to refuse the king? Unthinkable. There's no telling what he would do to her if she said no. On the other hand. . .she loved her husband. Yes, he was gone a lot, and yes, she was lonely. But adultery? She didn't know if she could go through with it.

The scriptures don't tell us whether or not Bathsheba believed in or followed God's laws, but they do tell us what happened after she and David spent the night together. First, she got pregnant. Then David had her husband killed. And finally, after the proper time of mourning, she married and moved in with the king. But their deception was found out, and the child died. Sin gave way to death, as it always does. Mortified at what they'd done, David and Bathsheba grieved.

But God used a horrible situation to complete His mighty plan. David and Bathsheba conceived another baby, and he was called Solomon, "God's Beloved." This child became king after David's death, rebuilt the temple in Jerusalem, and wrote several books of the Bible. He was known as the wisest man who ever lived.

From gory death to glorious wealth—that kind of turnaround is God's specialty. After all, left to our own devices, we can create huge messes.

Mothers know all about messes, don't we? We deal with them from the moment we wake up to the minute our head hits the pillow. And our mom-DNA causes us to try and fix them. But let's be honest. Some messes, like the one David and Bathsheba made, can't be cleaned up easily. When we lose a job due to our own negligence, when our husband tells us he is filing for a divorce, when our child gets jail time—we need someone bigger than us who can come and pick up the pieces.

Guess what? Messes run all through the Bible. From Adam and Eve's disastrous disobedience to the Apostle Saul's persecutions of Christians (before he met Jesus for himself), most biblical characters dealt with their own sinful choices and man-made predicaments. And yet, God used each one to tell His story. He redeemed their ugly messes and wove a beautiful tapestry out of them.

What a relief! Mom, you don't have to have it all together. God loves you right where you are, and He wants to love, forgive, and restore you. So stop trying to clean up your own messes—and start leaning on Jesus.

Think It Over

- What "messy" Bible characters do you identify with, and why?

- What messes in your life need to be cleaned up?

- Are you willing to hand them over to God, to see what He—and He alone—can do?

For his anger lasts only a moment, but his favor lasts a lifetime; weeping may remain for a night, but rejoicing comes in the morning.
PSALM 30:5 NIV

Failures as Fodder
Bathsheba (Part 2)
Abridged from 2 Samuel 12 NLV

Then the Lord sent Nathan to David. He came to him and said, "There were two men in one city. One was rich and the other was poor. The rich man had many flocks and cattle. But the poor man had nothing except one little female lamb which he bought and fed. It grew up together with him and his children. It would eat his bread and drink from his cup and lie in his arms. It was like a daughter to him.

Now a traveler came to the rich man. But the rich man was not willing to take from his own flock or his own cattle, to make food for the traveler who had come to him. Instead, he took the poor man's female lamb and made it ready for the man who had come to him."

David was very angry at the man, and said to Nathan, "As the Lord lives, for sure the man who has done this should die. And he must pay four times the worth of the lamb, because he did this thing without pity."

Nathan said to David, "You are the man! This is what the Lord God of Israel says: 'I chose you to be the king of Israel. I saved you from the hand of Saul. I gave you Saul's family and Saul's wives into your care. I gave you the nations of Israel and Judah. And if this were too little, I would give you as much more. Why have you hated the Word of the Lord by doing what is bad in His eyes? You have killed Uriah the Hittite with the sword. You have taken his wife to be your wife. You have killed him with the sword of the sons of Ammon.'"

"So now some from your family, even in the future, will die by the sword, because you have turned against Me and have taken the wife of Uriah the Hittite to be your wife. This is what the Lord says: 'See, I will bring trouble against you from your own family. I will take your wives in front of your eyes and give them to your neighbor. He will lie with your wives in the light of day. You did it in secret. But I will do this in front of all Israel, and under the sun.'"

Then David said to Nathan, "I have sinned against the Lord." And Nathan said to him, "The Lord has taken away your sin. You will not die. But by this act you have given those who hate the Lord a reason to speak against the Lord. The child that is born to you will die for sure."

Then Nathan went home.

The Lord sent trouble upon the child of Uriah's wife and David, so that he was very sick. David begged God to make the child well. He went without food and lay all night on the ground. The leaders of his family stood beside him to lift him up from the ground. But David was not willing. He would not eat food with them. The child died on the seventh day. . . . Then David comforted his wife Bathsheba. He went in and lay with her, and she gave birth to a son. He gave him the name Solomon. The Lord loved him.

Failures as Fodder
Bathsheba (Part 2)
Life Application

Bathsheba's life could be considered a failure. After all, she slept with King David while her husband was at war, had a child from the illicit affair, and married David after he had her husband killed.

When their sins were exposed, Bathsheba and David repented, but their child became sick and died. The scriptures don't tell us much about how Bathsheba felt, but as a mother, she had to have been devastated.

But God wasn't done with Bathsheba. She bore Solomon, whom David chose to succeed him. And Solomon went on to build the temple, fulfilling a promise God had given to David. In Proverbs, we see Bathsheba again, advising Solomon on the qualities of a virtuous wife. She even advises him, speaking out of her own experience: "Don't waste your life chasing after women! This has ruined many kings."

Even more amazing is the fact that Solomon and the entire lineage of David were the ancestors of Jesus Christ, God's own Son. What the world saw as failure, God saw as fodder.

Bathsheba's story proves that God redeems even the most heinous sin. He loves to restore and rebuild, and His Word is the only final word in our lives. So don't let your past hold you back. God isn't done with you, either.

Mom, God can use your own failures as fodder in His mighty plan. Do you have things you're ashamed of? Ask God how He can redeem those things and make something better out of them.

Perhaps you could share about your own failings with your children, encouraging them to make better choices. Jinny, a mom of two tweens, does this and says that it helps her kids see her as human. She notes that sometimes her children can get discouraged by hard times, not realizing that everyone goes through rough patches. When Jinny shares her own "war stories," the children get a fresh view of their mother and gain the realization that sometimes God allows us to go through trials in order to form our character.

Are you afraid of what your kids will think if you share too much? Pray about the right way and time to bring things up. Go light on the details and speak in generalizations. Be sure to highlight God's redemption, and warn your children that the end doesn't justify the means.

If you're honest about your past, those you care about will still love you. Hopefully, they'll begin to realize that God, who is perfect, can take any situation and turn it around for His glory.

Think It Over

- What personal failures haunt you?

- How can you best share those experiences with your children and help them learn from your mistakes?

- How have you grown in character as a result of failing?

- In what ways does the story of Bathsheba encourage you?

"See, the former things have taken place,
and new things I declare; before they spring
into being I announce them to you."
ISAIAH 42:9 NIV

Strength to Do the Unthinkable
Bilhah
Abridged from Genesis 30, 35 NLV

When Rachel saw that she had not given birth to any children for Jacob, she became jealous of her sister. She said to Jacob, "Give me children, or else I am going to die!"

Then Jacob became angry with Rachel. He said, "Am I taking God's place? Who has kept you from giving birth?" Then she said, "Here is Bilhah, the woman who serves me. Go in to her, and let her give birth for me. Even I may have children through her." So she gave Bilhah to him for a wife, the woman who served her. . . . Bilhah. . .gave birth to a son. Then Rachel said, "God has done the right thing for me. He has heard my voice and has given me a son." So she gave him the name Dan. Bilhah. . .gave birth to another son for Jacob. So Rachel said, "I have fought a hard fight with my sister, and I have won." She gave him the name Naphtali. . . .

God said to [Jacob], "I am the All-powerful God. Have many children and add to your number. A nation and a group of nations will come from you. Kings will come from you. I will give you the land which I gave to Abraham and Isaac. This land I will give to your children and their children's children after you."

Then God went up from him in the place where He had spoken with him. Jacob set up a pillar of stone in the place where He had spoken with him. And he poured a drink offering and also oil on it. So Jacob gave the place where God had spoken with him the name Bethel.

Then they traveled from Bethel. When there was still a long way to go before coming to Ephrath, Rachel began to give birth. She suffered much pain. And while she was suffering, the woman who was helping her said to her, "Do not be afraid. For now you have another son." As Rachel's soul was leaving, for she died, she gave him the name Benoni. But his father gave him the name Benjamin. So Rachel died, and was buried on the way to Ephrath (that is, Bethlehem). Jacob set up a stone on her grave. And that is the stone of Rachel's grave to this day.

Then Israel traveled on, and put up his tent on the other side of the tall building of Eder. While Israel lived in that land, Reuben went and lay with Bilhah, the woman who acted as his father's wife. And Israel heard about it.

There were twelve sons of Jacob. The sons of Leah were Reuben, Jacob's first-born, then Simeon, Levi, Judah, Issachar, and Zebulun. The sons of Rachel were Joseph and Benjamin. The sons of Bilhah, the woman who served Rachel, were Dan and Naphtali. The sons of Zilpah, the woman who served Leah, were Gad and Asher. . . .

Jacob came to his father Isaac at Mamre of Kiriath-arba (that is, Hebron), where Abraham and Isaac had been living. Now Isaac had lived 180 years. And Isaac breathed his last and died, and was joined to his people who died before him.

Strength to Do the Unthinkable
Bilhah
Life Application

As a concubine, Bilhah had no rights. Rachel gave her to Jacob like the piece of property she was considered. Then Rachel raised—and even named—the children Bilhah bore. Jacob had several other wives, and she never knew when he would want her—or not want her. As Rachel's maidservant, she saw the way Jacob loved Rachel, and it must have hurt her deeply. At one point, Jacob even put Bilhah and her children on the front lines of what he was sure would be a big battle—while he put Rachel and her children near the back! Later, one of Leah's sons raped Bilhah, losing his inheritance as Jacob's eldest.

Humiliation and loneliness all seemed to plague Bilhah's life. Her name means *faltering* or *bashful* in Hebrew—a fitting description. Bilhah was nothing more than a slave, and each day, she woke up to an unthinkable situation. Wouldn't you falter if you had to endure such a life?

Sometimes God asks us as moms to do the unthinkable. He may ask you to love a family member who doesn't share your values. He might want you to stay in a job you don't enjoy, for little pay. Or He may tell you to unconditionally love and support a child who treats you as though you're the scum of the earth.

And we think, *Are you crazy, Lord? There's no way!*

The truth is, *He* is the way. For each difficulty, God provides His help. When others mock your faith, ask

Him for the strength to pray for them, instead of retaliating. When you're bored silly at work, ask Him for the motivation to see the bigger picture and do your job well. When your child insults you, tell God you need the patience to love him anyway.

Each daily challenge provides you the opportunity to ask God for His wisdom, courage, and endurance. Are you potty training a toddler? God can give you the perspective to see that this season will soon be over. Does your tween roll her eyes at every word you say? God will provide a sense of humor and will help you defuse a potentially volatile situation.

Today, whatever comes your way, resolve not to panic. Instead, take a deep breath and say, "Lord, help me." Then step back, and rest in this fact: God promises that when we ask for His help, He will show up—and show off.

Think It Over

- What impossible thing has God required of you?

- How could you let God provide in that situation?

- In what ways do you relate to Bilhah?

- What can her situation reveal to you?

> *"Blessed is she who has believed*
> *that what the Lord has said to*
> *her will be accomplished!"*
> LUKE 1:45 NIV

When God Takes Too Long
Elizabeth (Part 1)
Abridged from Luke 1 NLV

When Herod was king of the country of Judea, there was a Jewish religious leader named Zacharias. . . . His wife was of the family group of Aaron. Her name was Elizabeth. They were right with God and obeyed the Jewish Law and did what the Lord said to do. They had no children because Elizabeth was not able to have a child. Both of them were older people.

Zacharias was doing his work as a religious leader for God. The religious leaders were given certain kinds of work to do. Zacharias was chosen to go to the house of God to burn special perfume. Many people stood outside praying during the time the special perfume was burning.

Zacharias saw an angel of the Lord standing on the right side of the altar where the special perfume was burning. When he saw the angel, Zacharias was troubled and afraid.

The angel said to him, "Zacharias, do not be afraid. Your prayer has been heard. Your wife Elizabeth will give birth to a son. You are to name him John. You will be glad and have much joy. Many people will be happy because he is born. He will be great in the sight of the Lord and will never drink wine or any strong drink. Even from his birth, he will be filled with the Holy Spirit. Many of the Jews will be turned to the Lord their God by him. He will be the one to go in the spirit and power of Elijah before Christ comes. He will turn the hearts of the fathers back to their children. He will teach those who do not obey to be right with God. He will get people ready for the Lord" (Malachi 4:5-6).

Zacharias said to the angel, "How can I know this for sure? I am old and my wife is old also."

The angel said to him, "My name is Gabriel. I stand near God. He sent me to talk to you and bring to you this good news. See! You will not be able to talk until the day this happens. It is because you did not believe my words. What I said will happen at the right time."

The people outside were waiting. They were surprised and wondered why Zacharias stayed so long in the house of God. When he came out, he could not talk to them. They knew he had seen something special from God while he was in the house of God. He tried to talk to them with his hands but could say nothing. When his days of working in the house of God were over, he went to his home.

Some time later Elizabeth knew she was to become a mother. She kept herself hidden for five months. She said, "This is what the Lord has done for me. He has looked on me and has taken away my shame from among men."

When God Takes Too Long
Elizabeth (Part 1)
Life Application

Zacharias and Elizabeth served God faithfully, but they felt a gaping hole in the middle of their hearts. For years, they had longed for a child, but God hadn't granted their desire. And with them both approaching old age, it seemed as though He never would.

Elizabeth, like many priests' wives, often babysat other people's children while the parents met with her husband. As she rocked and sang to the babies, her heart ached. As she played hide-and-seek with the toddlers, she probably wiped away tears. And when she talked to the teenage girls, her mind may have wandered to the fact that she would never have a grandchild to dote on.

She loved the moments she shared with the children of the village, but she felt forgotten by God. Her prayers seemed whiny even to her. "Oh, God," she said over and over, "I know I'm too old to carry a child. But if You could bring one into our lives, some way, I would never ask You for anything again!"

Then she'd laugh at herself. *Foolish old woman*, she'd think. *God must have His reasons for leaving me childless. Surely He is sovereign, and He knows better than I do.* Still, her heart waited, and she never gave up hope. She knew that God had placed a strong desire in her to be a mother, and that in His way and time, He would change that desire—or fulfill it.

If you're like most moms, you hate to wait. After all, our whole culture has a fast-food mentality. We have minute rice, one-hour photo developing, same-day dry cleaning, and twenty-four-hour grocery stores. Do you want it right now? You can probably get it, depending on what "it" is.

However, if "it" is a satisfying job, an intimate relationship (with God, a mate, or a friend), a baby, a good prognosis, restored health, or financial stability—well, those things take time. And sometimes God's timing isn't what we expect.

Have you heard of Saint Augustine? He wrote more than a thousand books and shaped Christian history. But for four decades, his mother Monica prayed for her wild and wayward son to get serious with God.

Sometimes God seems silent at just the wrong time. We pray and wait. . .and wait some more. It can be frustrating—and exhausting.

But we simply can't see what God sees. He knows the end of the story, and we do not. Sometimes He asks us to wait because others (not necessarily us) are not ready for His answer. At other times, He may want to develop our faith.

The stories of waiting biblical moms like Elizabeth, Sarah, and Hannah teach us that God does hear our prayers, even if He seems like He's taking too long to answer. Whatever His reasons for the delay, we can trust His ways—and His timing.

Think It Over

- In what ways have you waited on God?

- Is it difficult for you to be patient?
  If so, how?

- In what situations have you realized God's
  timing was better than yours?

- What do you think God is saying to you
  through the story of Elizabeth?

> *For since the beginning of the world*
> *Men have not heard nor perceived by the ear,*
> *Nor has the eye seen any God besides You,*
> *Who acts for the one who waits for Him.*
> ISAIAH 64:4 NKJV

God as Our Strength
Elizabeth (Part 2)
Abridged from Luke 1 NLV

When Herod was king of the country of Judea, there was a Jewish religious leader named Zacharias. . . . His wife was of the family group of Aaron. Her name was Elizabeth. They were right with God and obeyed the Jewish Law and did what the Lord said to do. They had no children because Elizabeth was not able to have a child. Both of them were older people.

Zacharias was doing his work as a religious leader for God. The religious leaders were given certain kinds of work to do. Zacharias was chosen to go to the house of God to burn special perfume. Many people stood outside praying during the time the special perfume was burning.

Zacharias saw an angel of the Lord standing on the right side of the altar where the special perfume was burning. When he saw the angel, Zacharias was troubled and afraid.

The angel said to him, "Zacharias, do not be afraid. Your prayer has been heard. Your wife Elizabeth will give birth to a son. You are to name him John. You will be glad and have much joy. Many people will be happy because he is born. He will be great in the sight of the Lord and will never drink wine or any strong drink. Even from his birth, he will be filled with the Holy Spirit. Many of the Jews will be turned to the Lord their God by him. He will be the one to go in the spirit and power of Elijah before Christ comes. He will turn the hearts of the fathers back to their children. He will teach those who do not obey to be right with God. He will get people ready for the Lord" (Malachi 4:5–6).

When the time came, Elizabeth gave birth to a son. Her neighbors and family heard how the Lord had shown loving-kindness to her. They were happy for her. On the eighth day they did the religious act of the Jews on the child. They named him Zacharias, after his father. But his mother said, "No! His name is John."

They said to her, "No one in your family has that name."

Then they talked to his father with their hands to find out what he would name the child. He asked for something to write on. He wrote, "His name is John." They were all surprised and wondered about it. Zacharias was able to talk from that time on and he gave thanks to God. All those who lived near them were afraid. The news of what had happened was told through all the hill country of Judea. And all who heard those words remembered them and said, "What is this child going to be?" For the hand of the Lord was on him.

God as Our Strength
Elizabeth (Part 2)
Life Application

Elizabeth's shoulders shook as she sobbed. Her morning had been miserable—more than once, she had run outside to retch. The night before, she had tossed and turned and finally given up on rest. She could hardly breathe anymore, because the baby was situated so high in her womb. Her chest ached with heartburn, and her joints throbbed with pain.

The midwife said her pregnancy was going well—that a sick mother made for a healthy baby—so Elizabeth knew that the promised child in her womb would be fine. It was her own outcome she feared. *What made me think I could do this?* she asked herself. *I'm an old woman, after all!* All the years of barrenness had led her to form a perfect view of motherhood, from conception on. And now she was getting her first dose of reality.

Motherhood was going to be difficult, and her age would complicate things. A newborn didn't sleep much—she knew that. How would she and Zacharias survive so many sleepless nights?

But just as she was about to go crazy with anxiety, a familiar voice soothed her spirit. *Elizabeth,* the Holy Spirit whispered to her heart, *trust Jehovah. Lean on Jehovah. Rest in Him, and all will be well.*

"Of course," Elizabeth spoke aloud, her tears receding. She'd forgotten that God gave her this child in answer to her most fervent prayers. He would not leave or forsake her. He would give her strength.

More women are postponing marriage, whether to jump-start a career or because they want to marry later in life. And that means that more women are becoming moms in their late thirties and early forties. These midlife moms deal with a variety of issues—from lack of energy to fear of the future.

But they also have much to offer their kids. Through varied life experiences, they bring a maturity and "been there, done that" kind of wisdom to mothering that younger mothers sometimes don't have. Older moms tend to relax and enjoy their children because they've waited so long to have babies.

Also, a number of today's grandparents are raising their grandchildren for one reason or another, and many of them are having a ball. Those children are blessed to have older, wiser guardians, who know that some things aren't worth worrying about and that children grow up too fast.

It's nice to know that God doesn't put an age limit on mothering. In fact, His Word is full of older-than-expected moms who relied on Him for energy, wisdom, and grace.

Whatever your age, remember that God gave you children, and He will not leave or forsake you. Lean on Him, rest in Him, and trust Him to help you. He can give you the strength you need.

Think It Over

- What do you think are some of the issues older moms face?

- If you know an older parent, think of some ways you could encourage her.

- Regardless of your age, what parts of motherhood are difficult for you?

- Write verses about God never leaving or forsaking you on index cards and place them around your home. Meditate on them throughout your day, and see what a difference it makes.

"Haven't I commanded you? Strength! Courage! Don't be timid; don't get discouraged. God, your God, is with you every step you take."
JOSHUA 1:9 MSG

A Life of Highs and Lows
Eve
Abridged from Genesis 2–4 NLV

Then the Lord God made man from the dust of the ground. And He breathed into his nose the breath of life. Man became a living being. The Lord God planted a garden to the east in Eden. He put the man there whom He had made. And the Lord God made to grow out of the ground every tree that is pleasing to the eyes and good for food. And He made the tree of life grow in the center of the garden, and the tree of learning of good and bad. . . .

Then the Lord God said, "It is not good for man to be alone. I will make a helper that is right for him. . . ." So the Lord God put the man to sleep as if he were dead. And while he was sleeping, He took one of the bones from his side and closed up the place with flesh. The Lord God made woman from the bone which He had taken from the man. And He brought her to the man. . . .

The woman saw that the tree was good for food, and pleasing to the eyes, and could fill the desire of making one wise. So she took of its fruit and ate. She also gave some to her husband, and he ate. . . .

Then the Lord God said to the woman, "What is this you have done?" And the woman said, "The snake fooled me, and I ate. . . ."

To the woman He said, "I will make your pain much worse in giving birth. You will give birth to children in pain. Yet your desire will be for your husband, and he will rule over you. . . ."

The man lay with his wife Eve and she was going to have a child and she gave birth to Cain. . . . Next she gave birth to his brother Abel. Now Abel was a keeper of sheep, but Cain was one who worked the ground.

The day came when Cain brought a gift of the fruit of the ground to the Lord. But Abel brought a gift of the first-born of his flocks and of the fat parts. The Lord showed favor to Abel and his gift. But He had no respect for Cain and his gift. So Cain became very angry and his face became sad. . . .

Then the Lord said to Cain, "Where is Abel your brother?"

And he said, "I do not know. Am I my brother's keeper?"

The Lord said, "What have you done? The voice of your brother's blood is crying to Me from the ground. Now you are cursed because of the ground, which has opened its mouth to receive your brother's blood from your hand. When you work the ground, it will no longer give its strength to you. You will always travel from place to place on the earth. . . ."

Then Cain went away from the face of the Lord, and stayed in the land of Nod, east of Eden.

A Life of Highs and Lows
Eve
Life Application

Eve had a life of extreme highs and lows. High: She awoke to find herself in a perfect paradise with a handsome man by her side. She walked in the garden, naked and unashamed, enjoying her own private zoo and a spontaneous, intimate relationship with both her husband and the Creator. What a deal!

Low: She listened to the serpent and ate of the forbidden tree, sending her life—and her mate's—into a spiral of regret, heartache, and hard work. No longer was she free from stress, able to spend her days happily roaming in the garden with her Maker and her soul mate. Instead, she and her husband were forced to labor for their food.

High: God gave her two sons, whom she loved. Low: The labor and delivery hurt like crazy, and the pregnancies weren't always a bed of roses, either! High: She nursed her boys and reveled in their differences. Low: Those differences led to fighting and jealousy, and in one swift blow, one of her sons killed the other. Can you imagine? After all the drama, Cain left the land where his parents lived and moved far away. Once, Eve enjoyed abundant life and a full heart. But when her eldest boy murdered his sibling, it must've torn Eve's world apart once again.

❧

The world is still a chaotic place, full of heartache and uncertainty. Life often feels like a roller coaster, with the highs and lows coming at women faster than our hearts can bear. The planet is full of suicide bombers, child abusers, and natural disasters. Even the "lesser" stresses—job difficulties, marital strife, and parental discipline challenges—wreak havoc on a mom's peace level. Fear can easily overwhelm us after we read the newspaper or listen to the radio. It would be easy to live in a state of constant anxiety.

So what's a concerned mom to do—freak out, move to a desert island, or put her head in the sand? None of those are good options.

Most moms can't control their circumstances, but they can control much of their environment. Today, take steps to fill your mind and heart with God's truth. By memorizing scripture and posting relevant verses around the house—on a bathroom mirror, on the fridge, by a computer, and in the car—you can surround yourself with the best weapon against fear.

Praise music is another great stress reliever. Why not play it in the house, at work, and in the car? Get some worship CDs to accompany your next workout. Other tips: Turn off the news and pick up the Word. Stop reading the newspaper. Reconsider the relationships you surround yourself with. Think about the words you say.

Women who control what comes in their mind and hearts aren't "Pollyannas" or out-of-touch optimists—they're smart. Changing your atmosphere can make a difference. Try it and see if your highs and lows don't just even out.

Think It Over

- In what ways do you identify with Eve?

- What life circumstances make you the most anxious?

- How do you usually deal with the anxiety?

- What are some healthier ways of dealing with it?

> *"You will keep him in perfect peace,*
> *whose mind is stayed on You,*
> *because he trusts in You."*
> Isaiah 26:3 nkjv

The God Who Sees
Hagar

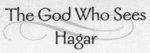

Abridged from Genesis 16, 21 NLV

Now Abram's wife Sarai had not given birth to any children. She had a woman servant from Egypt whose name was Hagar. So Sarai said to Abram, "Now see, the Lord has kept me from having children. Go in to the woman who serves me. It may be that I will get children through her."

Abram listened to what Sarai said. . . .

And when [Hagar] saw that she was going to have a child, she began to hate Sarai. Then Sarai said to Abram, "May the wrong done to me be upon you. I gave the woman who served me into your arms. But when she saw that she was going to have a child, she began to hate me. . . ."

So Sarai made it hard for Hagar. And Hagar ran away from her.

The angel of the Lord found Hagar by a well of water in the desert on the way to Shur. He said, "Hagar, you who serve Sarai, where have you come from and where are you going?" And she said, "I am running away from Sarai, the one I serve."

Then the angel of the Lord said to her, "Return to your boss. Put yourself under her power. . . ." The angel of the Lord also said to her, "See, you are going to have a child. And you will give birth to a son. You will give him the name Ishmael, because the Lord has heard how you have suffered. . . ."

So Hagar gave this name to the Lord Who spoke to her, "You are a God Who sees. . . ."

Hagar gave birth to Abram's son. And Abram gave his son who was born of Hagar the name Ishmael. . . .

Then the Lord visited Sarah as He had said and did for her as He had promised. Sarah was able to have a child and she gave birth to a son when Abraham was very old. He was born at the time the Lord said it would happen. Abraham gave the name Isaac to his son who was born to him by Sarah. . . . When the child grew old enough to stop nursing, Abraham made a special supper on that day.

But Sarah saw the son of Hagar the Egyptian make fun of Isaac. . . . So Sarah said to Abraham, "Put this woman servant and her son out of your home. The son of this woman servant will never get any of the riches of the family as will my son Isaac. . . ."

So Abraham got up early in the morning. He took bread and a leather bag of water, and gave it to Hagar, putting it on her shoulder. He gave her the boy, and sent her away. She left, and went from place to place in the desert in Beersheba.

When the water was gone, she put the boy under one of the bushes. Then she sat down as far away from him as an arrow flies. For she said, "Do not let me see the boy die." As she sat there, she cried a loud cry.

But God heard the voice of the boy. Then the angel of God called to Hagar from heaven, and said, "Why are you so troubled, Hagar? Do not be afraid. For God has heard the cry of the boy. Get up. Lift up the boy and hold him by the hand. For I will make a great nation of him."

Then God opened Hagar's eyes. And she saw a well of water. She went and filled the leather bag with water and gave the boy a drink.

The God Who Sees
Hagar
Life Application

Hagar always obeyed Sarah, whether the task was difficult or mundane. She had even slept with Abraham, gotten pregnant, and carried his son, Ishmael. For the most part, as long as Hagar kept a low profile, the two women got along fine.

When Sarah eventually had her own child, she kicked Hagar out for good, leaving Hagar to wander in the desert for a second time. Hagar's back ached, her mouth was full of dust, and her heart had never been heavier. She sat down to rest, wanting to cry but wondering if she had the strength.

Hagar drank one sip of her water and gave her baby the last of it. As he began to cry for more, she couldn't stop the tears. With gut-wrenching sobs, she cried out to God. "Oh, Lord God, please save us! I can't watch my son die!"

And God heard. With tender compassion, He opened her eyes and showed her a well. He saw her, just as He had when Sarah sent her away the first time—when an angel had appeared and told Hagar she was pregnant.

That story is the first time in scripture that the name "El Roi" is used for God. It means "The God who sees." God had never left Hagar's side, and He cared about what happened to her and her child.

What a comforting thought! *God sees.*

As moms, much of what we do goes unnoticed and

unappreciated. Although we have the most important job in the world, there are no award shows for stellar parenting skills. There's not an Olympics where mothers receive medals for "best diaper change" or "smartest disciplinary techniques" (but maybe there should be!).

Moms can begin to feel invisible after a while: The endless hours and thankless tasks can overwhelm us. Like Hagar, we can feel abandoned. *When will my needs get met?* we wonder in frustration. If we're not careful, we can become bitter and angry. *Look at all I do for this family*, we think. *And never a word of thanks!*

Don't forget, Mom: God notices. God sees. And He promises to meet our needs. When you're up in the middle of the night, rocking a sick baby, He's with you. When you rise early to fix healthy lunches before the kids are up, He applauds. When you listen to your teenage daughter's ranting and stay calm, He smiles. And He will reward you. Maybe not with a golden statuette, but with His presence and peace.

So ask Him for His perspective, and remind yourself that He delights in you. To Him, you're more than a medal winner. You're His trophy—and He loves to show you off to the angels in heaven. "See my daughter?" he says. "She's doing a great job!"

Think It Over

- What mom-related tasks cause you the most frustration?

- Do you sometimes feel unappreciated? How do you express that?

- What do you feel when you hear the phrase "El Roi" (the God who sees)?

- What does the story of Hagar mean to you?

"The LORD your God is with you,
he is mighty to save. He will take great delight
in you, he will quiet you with his love,
he will rejoice over you with singing."
ZEPHANIAH 3:17 NIV

God Can Be Trusted
Hannah (Part 1)

Abridged from 1 Samuel 1 NLV

There was a certain man from Ramathaim-zophim of the hill country of Ephraim. His name was Elkanah, the son of Jeroham, the son of Elihu, the son of Tohu, the son of Zuph, an Ephraimite. He had two wives. The name of one was Hannah. The name of the other was Peninnah. Peninnah had children, but Hannah had no children.

This man would go from his city each year to worship and to give gifts on the altar in Shiloh to the Lord of All. Eli's two sons, Hophni and Phinehas, were the Lord's religious leaders there. On the day when Elkanah killed animals on the altar in worship, he would give part of the gift to his wife Peninnah and to all her sons and daughters. But he would give twice as much to Hannah, for he loved Hannah. But the Lord had made it so she could not have children. . . .

Then Hannah stood up after they had eaten and drunk in Shiloh. Eli the religious leader was sitting on the seat by the door of the house of the Lord. Hannah was very troubled. She prayed to the Lord and cried with sorrow. Then she made a promise and said, "O Lord of All, be sure to look on the trouble of Your woman servant, and remember me. Do not forget Your woman servant, but give me a son. If You will, then I will give him to the Lord all his life. And no hair will ever be cut from his head."

While she kept praying to the Lord, Eli was watching

her mouth. Hannah was speaking in her heart. Her lips were moving, but her voice was not heard. So Eli thought she had drunk too much. Eli said to her, "How long will you be drunk? Put wine away from you."

But Hannah answered, "No, my lord, I am a woman troubled in spirit. I have not drunk wine or strong drink, but I was pouring out my soul to the Lord. Do not think of your woman servant as a woman of no worth. For I have been speaking out of much trouble and pain in my spirit."

Then Eli answered, "Go in peace. May the God of Israel do what you have asked of Him."

And Hannah said, "Let your woman servant find favor in your eyes." So she went her way and ate, and her face was no longer sad.

God Can Be Trusted
Hannah (Part 1)
Life Application

Hannah took a deep breath and tried to eat.

"What's wrong?" her husband asked.

"I don't feel like eating," she said.

Elkanah stood and walked over to her. Taking her hand, he said, "Can't you focus on our blessings? The Feast of Tabernacles is a time for celebrating." He motioned to the food on the table in front of them. Then he smiled and stroked Hannah's cheek with his thumb. "Besides, don't I mean more to you than ten sons?"

As she gazed at his face, which was full of compassion and concern, Hannah sighed. Why couldn't she be content with such a good man? Her eyes filling with tears, she pushed away from the table and ran to the temple.

Falling at the altar, she prayed fervently, as she had for many years. "Please," she begged, "let me have a baby. If You do, I will give him to You for as long as he lives!"

After her tears were spent, Hannah kept praying. Slowly, she began to feel better. And her spirit heard a soothing voice say, *I'm here. Be still. Be at peace.* As she loosened the grip on her desires and gave them to the Lord Almighty, she felt an assurance of a love much greater than her husband's. *Know I love you,* the voice said. *Know I'm listening.*

When Hannah got up from the altar, she didn't yet have an answer to her request, but she trusted the Lord enough to leave her problems with Him. For the first time in a long while, she was at peace.

Hannah knew two things: *God had heard her prayer*—she was confident that God would answer her, in His own way and timing—and *God could be trusted*. Hannah knew that the God who had created the universe could handle the fulfillment of her deepest longings.

Hannah's story in 1 Samuel 1 is the first time in the Bible that God is designated by the name "the Lord Almighty" or "the Lord of Hosts." The title is a general reference to the sovereignty of God over all powers in the universe.

How many times have we given our own problems—infertility, financial crises, fears, and doubts—to the Lord and then taken them back, convinced we can work them out on our own if we just tried harder? Often we say we believe in God's goodness, but we're afraid to surrender completely to Him. It's almost as if we believe He will require too much.

How much better our lives would be if we followed Hannah's example and left all our problems at the altar. After all, He is sovereign over all powers in the universe—and He can be trusted.

Precious Mom, choose to believe that God loves you. He is listening, and He has your best interests at heart. Rest in those facts, and be at peace.

Think It Over

- What unfulfilled longings do you have?

- How have those influenced your faith?

- Do you believe He listens, and that He can be trusted? Why or why not?

- What can you learn from Hannah's example?

*The prayer of a righteous [wo]man
is powerful and effective.*
JAMES 5:16 NIV

The Way to Let Go
Hannah (Part 2)

Abridged from 1 Samuel 1–2 NLV

The Lord made it possible for [Hannah] to have a child, and when the time came she gave birth to a son. She gave him the name Samuel, saying, "I have asked the Lord for him."

Then Elkanah went up with all those of his house to give the Lord the gift on the altar in worship as he did each year, and to pay what he had promised. But Hannah did not go. For she said to her husband, "I will not go up until the child no longer needs to be nursed. Then I will bring him before the Lord, to stay there forever."

Elkanah her husband said to her, "Do what you think is best. Stay here until he no longer needs to be nursed. Only may the Lord do as He has said."

So Hannah stayed and nursed her son until he no longer needed to be nursed. When she had finished nursing him, she took him with her to the house of the Lord in Shiloh, and the child was young. She brought a three year old bull, one basket of flour and a jar of wine also. Then they killed the bull, and brought the boy to Eli.

Hannah said [to Eli], "O, my lord! As you live, my lord, I am the woman who stood here beside you, praying to the Lord. I prayed for this boy, and the Lord has given me what I asked of Him. So I have given him to the Lord. He is given to the Lord as long as he lives." And they worshiped the Lord there.

Then Hannah prayed and said, "My heart is happy in the Lord. My strength is honored in the Lord. My mouth speaks with strength against those who hate me, because I have joy in Your saving power.

"There is no one holy like the Lord. For sure, there is no one other than You. There is no rock like our God. Speak no more in your pride. Do not let proud talk come out of your mouth. For the Lord is a God who knows. Actions are weighed by Him. The bows of the powerful are broken. But the weak are dressed in strength. Those who were full go out to work for bread. But those who were hungry are filled. She who could not give birth has given birth to seven. But she who has many children has become weak. The Lord kills and brings to life. He brings down to the grave, and He raises up. The Lord makes poor and makes rich. He brings low and He lifts up. He lifts the poor from the dust. He lifts those in need from the ashes. He makes them sit with rulers and receive a seat of honor. For what holds the earth belongs to the Lord. He has set the world in its place. He watches over the steps of His good people. But the sinful ones will be made quiet in darkness. For a man will not win by strength. Those who fight with the Lord will be broken to pieces. He will thunder in heaven against them. The Lord will decide about all people to the ends of the earth. He will give strength to His king. He will give power to His chosen one."

Elkanah went home to Ramah. But the boy served the Lord with Eli the religious leader.

The Way to Let Go
Hannah (Part 2)
Life Application

After hearing her many prayers mixed with tears, God blessed Hannah with Samuel, whose name means "asked of the Lord." Joy flooded her heart when she felt him kick inside her for the first time!

As the baby grew in her womb, Hannah thanked the Lord hundreds of times. Her heart almost burst when she heard Samuel's first sweet cries.

But as she stroked his face and smiled at him, her mind may have turned to the fact that she had promised him to the Lord. As she rocked him to sleep, did she regret her vow? As she nursed him, did she long to take it all back?

Whatever her feelings, Hannah kept her promise and, after Samuel was weaned, delivered the boy to the prophet Eli. Not only that, but she honored the prophet with a beautiful song of praise to her heavenly Father.

According to Israelite tradition, she visited her son only once a year. No doubt Hannah left a huge chunk of her heart behind as she waved good-bye to her tiny son.

But her arms were not empty for long, because God blessed Hannah with five more children. As Samuel grew up, he became a man of prayer and power from God.

What an incredible woman Hannah was. Her love for God was exemplified through her faith, steadfast prayer life, and commitment to follow through on her promises. Still, it could not have been easy to give up her firstborn, a direct answer to her heart's deepest longings. And just like Hannah, mothers today struggle with letting go.

Every day, we moms give up our children in small and large ways, leaving a part of our hearts with them every time. Moms let go a tiny bit when we leave our baby with a sitter for the first time. We surrender each time we wave good-bye to a toddler in a day care center. We leave some of our heart in the classroom when our child starts school. And we glance through the hands covering our eyes as our "babies" drive off in the family car—which will soon be packed with college gear.

Hannah is a great example of the way to let go. She shows us how we can face a slowly emptying nest with a balance of love and trust. The key is prayer.

First, we need to lay hands on our children's heads and cover them with fervent prayer. Then, to get rid of our paralyzing fear, we must take our hands off and raise them high, praising God for the gift of a child.

It's not easy, but it is simple. God will reward simple faith with His perfect peace.

Think It Over

• What prayers are you still waiting for God to answer?

• How do you express gratitude to God?

• Do you pray for and/or with your children? Why or why not?

• How comfortable are you with letting go of your kids?

> *"Don't let this throw you. You trust God, don't you? Trust me."*
> JOHN 14:1 MSG

An Ungodly Role Model
Herodias
Abridged from Mark 6 NLV

Jesus called the twelve followers to Him and began to send them out two by two. He gave them power over demons. He told them to take nothing along with them but a walking stick. They were not to take a bag or food or money in their belts. They were to wear shoes. They were not to take two coats. . . .

They preached that men should be sorry for their sins and turn from them. They put out many demons. They poured oil on many people that were sick and healed them.

King Herod heard about Jesus because everyone was talking about Him. Some people said, "John the Baptist has been raised from the dead. That is why he is doing such powerful works."

Other people said, "He is Elijah." Others said, "He is one who speaks for God like one of the early preachers."

When Herod heard this, he said, "It is John the Baptist, whose head I cut off. He has been raised from the dead." For Herod had sent men to take John and put him into prison. He did this because of his wife, Herodias. She had been the wife of his brother Philip. John the Baptist had said to Herod, "It is wrong for you to have your brother's wife." Herodias became angry with him. She wanted to have John the Baptist killed but she could not. Herod was afraid of John. He knew he was a good man and right with God, and he kept John from being hurt or killed. He liked to listen to John preach. But when he did, he became troubled.

Then Herodias found a way to have John killed. Herod gave a big supper on his birthday. He asked the leaders of the country and army captains and the leaders of Galilee to come. The daughter of Herodias came in and danced before them. This made Herod and his friends happy. The king said to the girl, "Ask me for whatever you want and I will give it to you." Then he made a promise to her, "Whatever you ask for, I will give it to you. I will give you even half of my nation."

She went to her mother and asked, "What should I ask for?"

The mother answered, "I want the head of John the Baptist. . . ."

Herod was very sorry. He had to do it because of his promise and because of those who ate with him. At once he sent one of his soldiers and told him to bring the head of John the Baptist. The soldier went to the prison and cut off John's head. He took John's head in on a plate and gave it to the girl. The girl gave it to her mother.

John's followers heard this. They went and took his body and buried it.

An Ungodly Role Model
Herodias
Life Application

Herod married his brother Philip's wife, Herodias, and when John the Baptist spoke out against the incest, Herodias was furious. Herodias had a beautiful daughter, Salome, who danced at Herod's birthday celebration. Dazzled, her stepfather pledged to give her whatever she wanted.

Salome breathlessly ran to her mother to report the offer. And that was all the opening Herodias needed. This original "Mommy Dearest" decided to use her daughter to carry out a devious plan. "Ask for John the Baptist's head," she said, and Salome obeyed.

Herod had promised Salome the world, and instead, she asked for a prophet's life. On his birthday, Herod succumbed to the evil schemes of his wife and stepdaughter. Instead of refusing them, he ordered his servants to kill John and bring him John's head on a platter.

If you look at the chain of sin that's going on in this saga, the pitfalls are pretty clear: Herodias sinned by marrying her husband's brother. Then, when John the Baptist called out the sin, she refused to repent and became angry instead with the person who pointed out her wrongdoing. Finally, she got revenge on God's prophet instead of falling to her knees and letting God forgive her. Worst of all, Herodias served as perhaps the single worst parenting role model in the Bible.

If you had godly parents, rejoice and give thanks. That legacy is a gift from God. If God didn't provide someone for you to emulate, your job is a little harder—but it's not impossible.

You can take several steps to ensure that you don't repeat the sins of the past. First, pray that God will help you forgive your parents for their mistakes. Instead of becoming bitter, you may need to work through your anger and grief with a godly counselor. Take as long as you need in this part of the process, because it's tough work. However, you'll find healing, joy, and freedom on the other side of your pain.

Second, commit to becoming the parent you wish you had. Take Christian parenting classes, find a support group, immerse yourself in scripture, and find mentors who can come alongside you and model godly parenting skills. Most of all, be diligent, and don't give up. It's worth it!

Third, forgive yourself when you mess up, because you will. Everyone does. But remember this, Mom: When you seek God's will, He will grant you wisdom and discernment. You can count on Him for patience, peace, and endurance.

Finally, remind yourself and your kids that our heavenly Father is the only perfect parent. Then your children will truly have what you didn't have, and you can stand back and be amazed at what He does in and through them—and you.

Think It Over

- In what ways were your parents good role models?

- In what ways were they poor parenting mentors?

- What steps can you take to keep yourself from making the same mistakes?

- If you had godly parents, send them a letter of appreciation—or if that's not possible, write a thank-you to God.

Be imitators of God, therefore, as dearly loved children and live a life of love, just as Christ loved us and gave himself up for us as a fragrant offering and sacrifice to God.
EPHESIANS 5:1–2 NIV

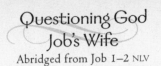

Questioning God
Job's Wife
Abridged from Job 1–2 NLV

There was a man in the land of Uz whose name was Job. That man was without blame. He was right and good, he feared God, and turned away from sin. Seven sons and three daughters were born to him. He had 7,000 sheep, 3,000 camels, 1,000 oxen, 500 female donkeys, and many servants. He was the greatest of all the men of the east. . . .

The Lord said to Satan, "Have you thought about My servant Job? For there is no one like him on the earth. . . ."

Then Satan answered the Lord, "Does Job fear God for nothing? Have You not made a wall around him and his house and all that he has, on every side? You have brought good to the work of his hands, and he has received more and more in the land. But put out Your hand now and touch all that he has. And for sure he will curse You to Your face."

Then the Lord said to Satan, "See, all that he has is in your power. Only do not put your hand on him. . . .

On a day when Job's sons and daughters were eating and drinking wine in their oldest brother's house, a man came to Job with news, saying, ". . .the Sabeans came and took [your livestock]. They also killed the servants with the sword. I alone have run away from them to tell you."

While he was still speaking, another man came and said, "The fire of God fell from heaven and burned up the sheep and the servants and destroyed them. I alone have gotten away to tell you."

While he was still speaking, another came and said, "The Babylonians divided into three groups and came to fight. They took the camels and killed the servants with the sword. I alone have gotten away to tell you."

While he was still speaking, another also came and said, "Your sons and daughters were eating and drinking wine in their oldest brother's house. And see, a strong wind came from the desert and hit the four corners of the house. It fell on the young people and they are dead. I alone have gotten away to tell you."

Then Job stood up and tore his clothing and cut the hair from his head. And he fell to the ground and worshiped. He said, "Without clothing I was born from my mother, and without clothing I will return. The Lord gave and the Lord has taken away. Praise the name of the Lord."

In all this Job did not sin or blame God. . . .

Satan answered the Lord and said, "Skin for skin! Yes, all that a man has he will give for his life. Put out Your hand now and touch his bone and his flesh, and he will curse You to Your face."

So the Lord said to Satan, "See, he is in your power. Only do not kill him."

Then Satan went out from the Lord. And he made very bad sores come on Job from the bottom of his foot to the top of his head. . . .

Then his wife said to him, "Do you still hold on to your faith? Curse God and die!"

But he said to her, "You speak as one of the foolish women would speak. Should we receive good from God and not receive trouble?" In all this Job did not sin with his lips.

Job's wife was in shock. In a few weeks, she and her husband had lost every single one of their ten children in a freak accident. In addition, they had suffered the loss of their livelihood with the destruction of hundreds of crops and thousands of heads of livestock. All their hopes and dreams—their very future—were gone in an instant.

Surely it's all just a bad dream, she must've thought. *I'll wake up, and this will have been a terrible nightmare.* But every day, she woke up to the same situation. Her days passed in a haze of grief, anger, and numbness. She felt cursed, and was quite sure her spouse's life was doomed. It was just a matter of time before she would lose him, too.

As she plodded through life, her limbs heavy from depression and lost hope, she began to question God. *What have we done to deserve this?* she probably thought. *My husband is righteous, and we've followed the law. He's even sacrificed on behalf of our children, just in case they sinned.* The questions came faster and faster. *Why are You toying with us? Why didn't You take me with my children? How can I go on living?*

Then the idea came to her. *Maybe it's something Job's done. Has he sinned and I don't know it? Has he broken some commandment that requires devastation to appease an angry God?*

When Job began suffering from a skin disease, she

knew God had played a cruel joke on them both. Her despair full-blown, she told Job to curse God and die. "You've already lost everything but your integrity," she said. "Just get it over with! Let Him take you, too!"

✌

Have you ever questioned God? As a mom, we hear questions all the time. Kids ask a lot of them. Some queries have easy answers: "Who made the world?" and "Why do we eat food?" Others are a little more difficult, like "Who made God?" and "Why is the sky blue?" Life has a lot of questions, too. Some have easy answers, like "Should I exercise?" and others don't, like "Why does God allow good people to suffer?"

Some people think it's wrong to question God. But in the Bible, God doesn't discourage curiosity. Later in the book that bears his name, Job has tons of things to ask his Maker. And in the New Testament, even Jesus asked, "My God, my God, why have You forsaken me?" from the cross.

Even God's Word doesn't have all the answers. Instead, it reminds us that God is bigger than we are and that His thoughts are far above our thoughts. Through His Word, He encourages those who believe in Him to seek Him, even when His ways are beyond our understanding. As the book of Job reveals, His focus is on developing a relationship with us, not satisfying our curiosity.

The next time you have questions, run to God—not away from Him. He promises to meet you there.

Think It Over

- What questions would you ask God if you could?

- In what ways have you dealt with doubt?

- Do you identify more with Job or his wife? Why?

- What can you learn from Job's response to suffering?

For no one is abandoned by the Lord forever.
Though he brings grief, he also shows compassion
because of the greatness of his unfailing love.
For he does not enjoy hurting people
or causing them sorrow.
LAMENTATIONS 3:31–33 NLT

The Bible's First Birth Mom
Jochebed

Abridged from Exodus 1–2 NLV

The sons of Israel had many children, and the people became many in number. There were so many that the land was filled with them.

Then a new king came into power over Egypt. . . . He said to his people, "See, the people of Israel are too many and too powerful for us. Come, let us be wise in how we act towards them, or they will become more in number. If there is a war, they might join with those who hate us. They might fight against us and then leave the land."

So they put men in power over them to make them work hard. . . . But the more the Egyptians made them suffer, the more they became until they spread throughout the land. So the Egyptians were afraid of the people of Israel. The Egyptians made the people of Israel work very hard. . . .

Then the king of Egypt spoke to the Hebrew nurses. . . . He said, "When you are helping the Hebrew women to give birth, and see the baby before the mother does, if it is a son, kill him. But if it is a daughter, let her live." But the nurses feared God. They did not do what the king of Egypt told them. They let the boys live.

So the king of Egypt called the nurses and said to them, "Why have you done this, and let the boys live?"

The nurses answered Pharaoh, "Because the Hebrew women are not like the Egyptian women. They are

strong. They give birth before the nurse comes to them."
So God was good to the nurses. And the people became many and strong. Because the nurses feared God, He gave them families.

Then Pharaoh told all his people, "Throw every son who is born to the Hebrews into the Nile. But keep every daughter alive."

Now a man of the family of Levi married a daughter of Levi. She was going to have a baby, and she gave birth to a son. When she saw that he was beautiful, she hid him for three months. But the time came when she could hide him no longer. So she took a basket made from grass, and covered it with tar and put the child in it. And she set it in the grass by the side of the Nile. His sister stayed to watch and find out what would happen to him.

Then the daughter of Pharaoh came to wash herself in the Nile. Her young women walked beside the Nile. She saw the basket in the tall grass and sent the woman who served her to get it. She opened it and saw the child. The boy was crying. She had pity on him and said, "This is one of the Hebrews' children."

Then his sister said to Pharaoh's daughter, "Should I go and call a nurse from the Hebrew women to nurse the child for you?"

Pharaoh's daughter said to her, "Go." So the girl went and called the child's mother. Then Pharaoh's daughter said to her, "Take this child away and nurse him for me. And I will pay you." So the woman took the child and nursed him. The child grew, and she brought him to Pharaoh's daughter. And he became her son. She gave him the name Moses, saying, "Because I took him out of the water."

The Bible's First Birth Mom
Jochebed
Life Application

Jochebed, Moses' mother, is the first real "birth mother" of the Bible. She had borne two other children, Miriam and Aaron, by the time Pharaoh issued his horrendous edict. And using all her God-given strength and creativity, Jochebed gave up her second son in order to save his life. How it must have grieved her to watch him grow up in another household—especially the home of the one who caused her pain in the first place!

Jochebed, like every birth mother, made a difficult, brave, heartbreaking choice. She trusted God and trusted another woman to bring up her child—knowing her decision was irrevocable. She heard Moses call another woman "mother," knowing that she had no alternative.

But God blessed the courage and resourcefulness of Jochebed. He used her son to lead His people out of slavery and into freedom. I'm sure that Jochebed was cheering on all the children of Israel from heaven as they made their miraculous exodus out of Egypt. Perhaps she even threw back her shoulders and said (as only a mother can): "That's my boy!"

❧

Birth moms who give their children up for adoption today have the same difficult choices to make as Jochebed did. Whether they are married, single, young, or old, they sacrifice raising their children in order to give them a better life. Birth moms feel their baby growing inside them—and bond with it—for nine months. However, once a birth mom delivers her baby, she begins to separate herself from the child. Some birth moms don't name their babies; others do. But each mom who gives her flesh and blood to another woman knows the grief of separation. She sees another woman cuddle and coo at her child, and her heart breaks.

Yet God blesses the courage and resourcefulness of birth moms, just as He blessed Jochebed's. By entrusting someone else (perhaps with better financial resources or a more solid family structure) with her child, a birth mom gives her child the greatest gift of all: a chance. She cheers her baby on from the sidelines, sometimes never seeing him again. But whether the adoption is open or closed, she can rest assured that God sees her sacrifice and will reward it.

After all, God Himself gave up His child, in order to give all of us a chance at eternal life. He knows the heartbreak of separation and the painful realities of letting someone else raise His most precious treasure. But He loved His other children (us) enough to take that risk.

And no doubt, when He sees a birth mom giving her child up, He says, "That's my girl!"

Think It Over

- How can the story of Jochebed encourage you as a mom?

- How did you choose your children's names?

- In what ways are you proud of your children?

He heals the brokenhearted and binds up their wounds. He determines the number of the stars and calls them each by name.
PSALM 147:3–4 NIV

A Servant Spirit
Keturah

Abridged from Genesis 15, 23, 25 NLV

The word of the Lord came to Abram in a special dream, saying, "Do not be afraid, Abram. I am your safe place. Your reward will be very great."

Then Abram said, "O Lord God, what will You give me? For I have no child. And the one who is to receive what belongs to me is Eliezer of Damascus." Abram said, "Because You have not given me a child, one born in my house will be given all I have."

Then the word of the Lord came to him, saying, "This man will not be given what is yours. But he who will come from your own body will be given what is yours." He took him outside and said, "Now look up into the heavens and add up the stars, if you are able to number them." Then He said to him, "Your children and your children's children will be as many as the stars."

Then Abram believed in the Lord, and that made him right with God.

God said to him, "I am the Lord Who brought you out of Ur of the Chaldeans to give you this land for your own."

And Abram said, "O Lord God, how may I know that it will be mine?". . .

When the sun was going down, Abram went into a sleep as if he were dead. And much fear and darkness came upon him. God said to Abram, "Know for sure that your children and those born after them will be strangers in a land that is not theirs. There they will be servants and suffer for 400 years. But I will punish the nation they will serve. And later they will come out with many riches. You will live many years, die in peace and be buried. . . ."

Sarah lived 127 years. . . . Then Sarah died in Kiriath-arba (that is, Hebron) in the land of Canaan. And Abraham had sorrow for Sarah and cried for her. . . .

Abraham took another wife whose name was Keturah. She gave birth to his sons, Zimran, Jokshan, Medan, Midian, Ishbak, and Shuah. Jokshan became the father of Sheba and Dedan. The sons of Dedan were Asshurim, Letushim, and Leummim. The sons of Midian were Ephah, Epher, Hanoch, Abida, and Eldaah. All these were the sons of Keturah.

A Servant Spirit
Keturah
Life Application

When Keturah's father told her he had arranged for her to be married, she was thrilled. But when he revealed that her chosen spouse was Abraham, her heart probably sank. Sure, Abraham was wealthy, but he was old. Very, very old.

And then there was Sarah, Abraham's late wife: Sarah's spunky, resilient faith in God, the miracle of Isaac's birth, and her sense of humor in the face of a unique parenting challenge (she was ninety-plus when she bore Isaac) had been told and retold for years in their village. How could Keturah hope to measure up to a local legend?

But on their wedding day, Abraham may have said something to his bride that changed everything. "The Lord promised me peace in my later years. And your name means 'myrrh,' a delightful fragrance. I know God has blessed me with you, Keturah, because your gentle spirit will bring a delightful, peaceful fragrance into our home."

From that day on, Keturah may have felt better about her marriage. It was still tough to be married to a man so much older than she—he could have been her grandfather!—but she found purpose in the midst of the difficulties. As she bore, fed, and served six sons to Abraham, she knew God had given her an opportunity to be a part of the incredible legacy of a great man of God.

Today, with so many marriages ending in divorce, modern families are more blended than ever before. And like Keturah, second wives have to deal with their own feelings of insecurity. A first wife's influence—whether positive or negative—can be overwhelming in a marriage, especially in the beginning. And it doesn't help when others compare a second wife's parenting and personality styles to the first wife.

So what's a second wife to do? The answer is simple, but not easy: Remember that we serve God and not men. Those who criticize don't know you, your family, or your relationship to God.

If you spend time with the Lord, and strive to let Him live through you as you serve your family, you can rest assured that He is pleased…and He will give you peace. Instead of worrying about what other people think or trying to "live up" to someone else's legacy, keep your heart pointed toward heaven, and ask Him to show you the way to live.

Also, realize you're not alone. The example of Keturah can point us toward developing a servant spirit, one that will bless our children, husbands, and everyone who comes in contact with us. Whether we're part of a blended family or not, we can bring a fragrance of peace and delight into our homes by letting Christ shine and serve through us.

Think It Over

- What unique parenting challenges do you face?

- What makes you insecure?

- How can you keep your heart pointed toward heaven?

- How can you serve your family with a spirit of graciousness this week?

*But thanks be to God, who always leads us
in triumphal procession in Christ and through
us spreads everywhere the fragrance
of the knowledge of him.*
2 CORINTHIANS 2:14 NIV

Glowing from the Inside Out
Leah (Part 1)
Abridged from Genesis 29 NLV

Jacob. . .completed [Leah's] wedding week. And Laban gave him his daughter Rachel as his wife. Laban also took Bilhah, a woman who served him, and gave her to his daughter Rachel, to serve her. So Jacob went in to Rachel also. He loved Rachel more than Leah. And he worked for Laban seven years more.

When the Lord saw that Leah was not loved, He made her able to give birth. But Rachel could not give birth. Leah was able to have a child and she gave birth to a son. She gave him the name Reuben. For she said, "The Lord has seen my trouble. Now my husband will love me." Then she was going to have another child and she gave birth to a son. She said, "The Lord has given me this son also, because He has heard that I am not loved." So she gave him the name Simeon. She was going to have another child and she gave birth to a son. She said, "Now this time my husband will be joined to me because I have given birth to his three sons." So she gave him the name Levi. She was going to have another child and she gave birth to a son. And she said, "This time I will praise the Lord." So she gave him the name of Judah. Then she stopped giving birth.

Glowing from the Inside Out
Leah (Part 1)
Life Application

Laban had two daughters, Leah and Rachel. Leah, the oldest, wasn't as attractive as her younger sister. Yet, the oldest usually married first. So when Jacob asked Laban for Rachel's hand in marriage, he agreed, but then he decided to deceive Jacob. Earlier, Jacob had tricked his father and deprived his own older brother of a blessing, so it seems ironic—and quite fitting—that he would be on the receiving end of a "bait and switch."

On Jacob and Rachel's wedding night, Laban went back on his promise and gave Leah to Jacob. And whether or not Leah helped plan the deception (the Bible doesn't reveal that juicy tidbit), the damage was done. Jacob might have been married to her, but he didn't love her. And Jacob *still* married Rachel.

Leah was now married to a man who didn't love her, and his other wife was her younger, more beautiful sister. He also had the right to sleep with Rachel and Leah's servants, who could give him children. Though Leah was fertile (a very big deal in those days), she wasn't loved.

To put it mildly, Leah was in a tough spot. Love brings out the best in people, especially women. When we're truly, deeply loved, we glow, and our inner beauty shines, making us more outwardly attractive. As the lesser-loved wife, what did Leah think of herself? Did she wish she were prettier—like her sister? How about you, Mom? Been there, done that? After all, we live in a culture that's obsessed with beauty, and the standard of what's attractive keeps changing as styles change. Television shows and magazine covers show celebrity moms who lose their baby weight seemingly overnight. Advertisements feature stick-thin models, and designers create clothes for only those women who have time and money for personal chefs and trainers. . . or great genes.

The pressure to be perfect has led to an epidemic of anorexia and bulimia, as well as a huge increase in the number of women getting plastic surgery. Sixteen-year-olds are even asking for breast implants as a birthday present—and parents are giving them!

Moms who want to look perfect are setting themselves up for failure and insecurity. Besides children taking up enormous amounts of time, they change a woman's body. Once you have a child, it's much harder (read "impossible") to achieve the goal of a flat tummy and tight thighs.

It's okay to want to look your best and be healthy, but be careful not to get caught up in the lie that your value lies in how good you look. Instead, choose to believe the Word of God, which says that your Creator truly, deeply loves you, whether or not you have thin thighs or white teeth. He delights in you from the top of your head to the bottom of your feet. When you let that reality sink in, your inner beauty will shine. You'll glow, girl!

Think It Over

- Do you identify with Leah? If so, how?

- What things do you like best about yourself?

- What things do you like least about yourself?

- Name some ways you could remind yourself daily that God loves you, just as you are.

But GOD told Samuel, "Looks aren't everything. Don't be impressed with his looks and stature. I've already eliminated him. GOD judges persons differently than humans do. Men and women look at the face; GOD looks into the heart."
1 SAMUEL 16:7 MSG

Insecure Moms
Leah (Part 2)

Abridged from Genesis 29 NLV

So Jacob worked seven years for Rachel. It was only like a few days to him, because of his love for her.

Then Jacob said to Laban, "Give me my wife so I may go in to her. For my time is finished." And Laban gathered all the men of the place together, and made a special supper. But in the evening he took his daughter Leah to him. Jacob went in to her. Laban also took Zilpah, a woman who served him, and gave her to his daughter Leah, to serve her.

When the morning came, Jacob saw that it was Leah. He said to Laban, "What have you done to me? Did I not work for you for Rachel? Why have you fooled me?"

Laban said, "It is not allowed in our country to give the younger in marriage before the first-born. Complete the wedding week of this one. Then we will give you the other one also if you work for me seven years more."

Jacob did so and completed her wedding week. And Laban gave him his daughter Rachel as his wife. Laban also took Bilhah, a woman who served him, and gave her to his daughter Rachel, to serve her. So Jacob went in to Rachel also. He loved Rachel more than Leah. And he worked for Laban seven years more.

Insecure Moms
Leah (Part 2)
Life Application

Leah played second fiddle to her more attractive sister all her life. The Bible says she had "weak eyes," which means she wasn't much to look at. And her cousin Jacob took one look at Rachel and fell hopelessly in love. Laban first promised Jacob he could marry the younger sister, but then conspired to pull a "switcheroo" on Jacob and Rachel's wedding night.

One wonders whether or not Leah enjoyed that night. When Jacob whispered endearments, did she cringe, knowing that his words were meant for her sister? Or did she pretend that the words of love were real? Did she enjoy his attention, knowing that for one night, she wasn't second-best, at least in Jacob's mind?

When Jacob woke up with Leah though, her illusions were shattered. His anger shocked her back into reality. For a week, Leah had her husband to herself, but after seven days, she had to share him with Rachel and their two maidservants as well. Second fiddle again.

Mom, do you feel like you play second fiddle? As you look around at other mothers, do you feel insecure and even inferior? Maybe you're a stay-at-home mom, and you compare yourself to the working mom who seems to have it all together. Her kids always look clean and happy, she wears the latest styles, and her wardrobe isn't spotted with spit-up. She contributes to the family's income, yet she doesn't seem stressed out by her career.

Or maybe you're that working mom. You appear to

juggle your roles well, and most days you do okay. But at times, you look longingly at the mom who drives car pools, plans class parties, and makes homemade dinners each night. She has fellow mom friends, and your phone only holds work contacts. Your laundry pile resembles Mount Everest, and your kids complain that you're always working. Your family needs your income, but you wonder if the grass is greener on the stay-at-home side.

It's too easy to compare our station in life to others and to feel second-best. The only solution is to keep our eyes on God and what He has called us to do. We don't know the reality behind other moms' situations. The "perfect-looking" working mom might feel frustrated that she has to log long hours at the office. The happy homemaker may feel lonely in her marriage.

Why not stop comparing, and pray instead for your fellow moms? Reach out by talking to them. You probably have more in common than you think. You might even find a new friend—and a renewed perspective on "having it all."

Think It Over

• Do you relate to the story of Leah? If so, how?

• When you compare yourself to other moms, what do you say about them—and about yourself?

• How does insecurity crop up in your life? Have you ever prayed about it?

Just as iron sharpens iron, friends
sharpen the minds of each other.
PROVERBS 27:17 CEV

Raising Christ-Followers
Lois and Eunice
Abridged from 2 Timothy 1 NLV

This letter is from Paul, a missionary of Jesus Christ. God has sent me to tell that He has promised life that lasts forever through Christ Jesus. I am writing to you, Timothy. You are my much-loved son. May God the Father and Christ Jesus our Lord give you His loving-favor and loving-kindness and peace.

I thank God for you. I pray for you night and day. I am working for God the way my early fathers worked. My heart says I am free from sin. When I remember your tears, it makes me want to see you. That would fill me with joy. I remember your true faith. It is the same faith your grandmother Lois had and your mother Eunice had. I am sure you have that same faith also.

For this reason, I ask you to keep using the gift God gave you. It came to you when I laid my hands on you and prayed that God would use you. For God did not give us a spirit of fear. He gave us a spirit of power and of love and of a good mind.

Do not be ashamed to tell others about what our Lord said, or of me here in prison. I am here because of Jesus Christ. Be ready to suffer for preaching the Good News and God will give you the strength you need. He is the One Who saved us from the punishment of sin. He is the One Who chose us to do His work. It is not because of anything we have done. But it was His plan from the beginning that He would give us His loving-favor through Christ Jesus. We know about it now because of the coming of Jesus Christ, the One Who saves.

He put a stop to the power of death and brought life that never dies which is seen through the Good News. I have been chosen to be a missionary and a preacher and a teacher of this Good News. For this reason, I am suffering. But I am not ashamed. I know the One in Whom I have put my trust. I am sure He is able to keep safe that which I have trusted to Him until the day He comes again.

Keep all the things I taught you. They were given to you in the faith and love of Jesus Christ. Keep safe that which He has trusted you with by the Holy Spirit Who lives in us.

Raising Christ-Followers
Lois and Eunice
Life Application

Paul led Timothy; his mother, Eunice; and grandmother, Lois; to Christ. But Timothy's foundation had already been set by these two God-fearing Jewish women. Since he was a baby, the duo had taught their charge the scriptures and filled his young mind with glorious stories about his heritage as one of God's chosen people. As he grew, so did his faith. And after Paul shared his own story with them, Timothy and his family believed in the risen Messiah. Later, Timothy willingly followed a call to evangelize his fellow Jews and began traveling with Paul on his missionary travels.

Scripture makes no mention of Timothy's father or grandfather, and they may have died when the boy was young. Ultimately, God provided Paul as a spiritual father to Timothy. The apostle gave guidance, accountability, and prayer support to Timothy, and in return, Timothy encouraged his mentor and provided him with companionship.

What an encouragement to single moms who desire to bring up their children in the fear of the Lord! Timothy's fervent faith reminds us that while it's beyond difficult to parent alone, a prayerful and intentional single mother *can* have a lasting impact on her children. And our heavenly Father, in His mercy and grace, will provide godly men to fill in relational gaps.

So how can mothers in our current culture raise their children to be godly young men and women? Here are just a few ideas: First, pray over them and read scripture with them. Each time you lift up their needs and/or impart biblical truth, you're making deposits in their spiritual "bank." Remember that—as the book of James attests—the fervent prayer of a righteous [wo]man accomplishes great things.

Second, be aware of the way media—books, television shows, the Internet, movies, or music—affects your kids. Be diligent to check out the artists and songs your kids are "into." Preview television shows and movies before letting them into your home. And don't be afraid to be strict or protective. That's your job!

Third, get as involved as you can with your child's school. Talk to teachers and other parents, and ask all sorts of questions about what your kids are learning. At home, bring up tough subjects and give a biblical viewpoint.

Finally, get to know your kids' friends (and their parents), and make your home a welcoming place. Host get-togethers and sleepovers, where you can control what happens.

But know this: Even the most diligent, prayerful parent can have children who choose to go their own way. In the end, we must give our children's futures to God, and pray that they follow hard after Him. Bottom line? We do the best we can, and leave the rest to Him.

Think It Over

- How have your ancestors influenced your parenting?

- Do you have godly role models you can look up to as a mom? If not, where could you find one?

- What are your concerns about raising godly children in today's culture?

- What is one thing you could start doing to help your kids form a biblical worldview?

*The Fear-of-God builds up confidence,
and makes a world safe for your children.*
PROVERBS 14:26 MSG

The Necessity of Support Groups
Mary, Mother of Jesus (Part 1)

Abridged from Luke 1 NLV

Gabriel was sent from God to Nazareth. Nazareth was a town in the country of Galilee. He went to a woman who had never had a man. Her name was Mary. She was promised in marriage to a man named Joseph. Joseph was of the family of David.

The angel came to her and said, "You are honored very much. You are a favored woman. The Lord is with you. You are chosen from among many women."

When she saw the angel, she was troubled at his words. She thought about what had been said. The angel said to her, "Mary, do not be afraid. You have found favor with God. See! You are to become a mother and have a Son. You are to give Him the name Jesus. He will be great. He will be called the Son of the Most High. The Lord God will give Him the place where His early father David sat. He will be King over the family of Jacob forever and His nation will have no end."

Mary said to the angel, "How will this happen? I have never had a man."

The angel said to her, "The Holy Spirit will come on you. The power of the Most High will cover you. The holy Child you give birth to will be called the Son of God.

"See, your cousin Elizabeth, as old as she is, is going to give birth to a child. She was not able to have children before, but now she is in her sixth month. For God can do all things."

Then Mary said, "I am willing to be used of the Lord. Let it happen to me as you have said." Then the angel went away from her.

At once Mary went from there to a town in the hill country of Judea. She went to the house of Zacharias to see Elizabeth. When Elizabeth heard Mary speak, the baby moved in her body. At the same time Elizabeth was filled with the Holy Spirit.

Elizabeth spoke in a loud voice, "You are honored among women! Your Child is honored! Why has this happened to me? Why has the mother of my Lord come to me? As soon as I heard your voice, the baby in my body moved for joy. You are happy because you believed. Everything will happen as the Lord told you it would happen."

Then Mary said, "My heart sings with thanks for my Lord. And my spirit is happy in God, the One Who saves from the punishment of sin. The Lord has looked on me, His servant-girl and one who is not important. But from now on all people will honor me. He Who is powerful has done great things for me. His name is holy. . . . He promised He would do this to our early fathers and to Abraham and to his family forever."

Mary stayed with Elizabeth about three months. Then she went to her own home.

The Necessity of Support Groups—
Mary, Mother of Jesus (Part 1)
Life Application

Most scholars agree that Mary was just a teenager when Gabriel visited her to tell her that God had chosen her to be the mother of the Messiah. This mere child suddenly had the world's salvation dependent on her. Wow!

Besides her age, her reaction to the angel's news was extraordinary. She humbly surrendered to God's plan, even though she was unsure and frightened. Still, she had to have questions and concerns.

What was she thinking after the angel left? Did she realize what was at stake? Did she want to recant, to refuse God? Did she wonder what Joseph, her parents, and her friends would think?

It's telling that Mary visited Elizabeth soon after the angel revealed the miracle growing inside her. Did her mother not offer support, counsel, or advice? We have no way of knowing. Maybe Mary's mom urged her to visit the older woman in order to protect her daughter. Perhaps Mary herself felt anxious to leave her small town, in case rumors started flying. Or maybe she was desperate for companionship in her mothering journey, and she knew that Elizabeth would freely give it.

The way Mary ran to Elizabeth shows that their relationship was close, and that she trusted her cousin to guide and encourage her. And whether or not she sought it, Mary received mentoring from the older pregnant woman.

Every mom needs her own support system. Fellow

moms and older, more experienced mothers provide conversation, fellowship, and sanity breaks in the midst of raising children.

The mothers that came before us had quilting circles, church potluck suppers, and front porches. Most of us don't have those things—and if you do, count yourself blessed! But whether we're aware of it or not, we need other moms. If we're not careful, we can run from school to church to soccer practice and never have a conversation that goes deeper than "I'm fine. How are you?" Soon, our souls get parched, and we feel disconnected from life.

Formal mom support groups like MOPS (Mothers of Preschoolers), Moms in Touch, and The M.A.W. (Mothers and Wives) Club hold regular meetings in communities around the world. Each organization has its own personality and purpose, but they're all meeting a mom's needs for connection and community.

Are you involved in a moms' group? If not, why not join one? If you don't find a group that suits you, pray about starting your own. Then keep your eye out for likeminded moms at the playground, school, and church. As you begin to connect with other women who understand your unique situation, you won't feel as alone anymore, and you'll realize that you're doing a better job than you thought after all.

Think It Over

- What needs do you have as a mom?

- How are those needs met regularly?

- What kind of support system do you have?

- Are you willing to join, or create, a moms' group? Why or why not?

Two are better than one, because they have a good return for their work: If one falls down, his friend can help him up. But pity the man who falls and has no one to help him up!
ECCLESIASTES 4:9–10 NIV

No Matter the Cost
Mary, Mother of Jesus (Part 2)

Abridged from Luke 3, 4, 8, 11 NLV

Jesus was about thirty years old when He began His work. People thought Jesus was the son of Joseph. . . . Jesus came to Nazareth where He had grown up. As He had done before, He went into the Jewish place of worship on the Day of Rest.

Then He stood up to read. Someone handed Him the book of the early preacher Isaiah. He opened it and found the place where it was written, "The Spirit of the Lord is on Me. He has put His hand on Me to preach the Good News to poor people. He has sent Me to heal those with a sad heart. He has sent Me to tell those who are being held that they can go free. He has sent Me to make the blind to see and to free those who are held because of trouble. He sent Me to tell of the time when men can receive favor with the Lord" (Isaiah 61:1–2).

Jesus closed the book. Then He gave it back to the leader and sat down. All those in the Jewish place of worship kept their eyes on Him. Then He began to say to them, "The Holy Writings you have just heard have been completed today."

They all spoke well of Jesus and agreed with the words He spoke. They said, "Is not this the son of Joseph?"

He said to them, "I wonder if you will tell this old saying to Me, 'Doctor, heal Yourself. What You did in the city of Capernaum, do in Your own country!' " He said, "A man who speaks for God is not respected in his own country. It is true that there were many women whose husbands had died in the Jewish land when Elijah lived. For three and a half years there was no rain and there was very little food in the land. Elijah was sent to none of them, but he was sent to a woman in the city of Zarephath in the land of Sidon. This woman's husband had died. There were many people in the Jewish land who had a bad skin disease when the early preacher Elisha lived. None of them was healed. But Naaman from the country of Syria was healed."

All those in the Jewish place of worship were angry when they heard His words. They got up and took Jesus out of town to the top of a high hill. They wanted to throw Him over the side. But Jesus got away from among them and went on His way. . . .

The mother of Jesus and His brothers came to Him. They could not get near Him because of so many people. Someone said to Jesus, "Your mother and brothers are standing outside. They want to see You."

Jesus said to them, "My mother and brothers are these who hear the Word of God and do it. . . ."

As Jesus was talking, a woman of the group said with a loud voice, "The woman is happy who gave You birth and who fed You."

But He said, "Yes, but those who hear the Word of God and obey it are happy."

No Matter the Cost
Mary, Mother of Jesus (Part 2)
Life Application

As Mary held Jesus in her arms for the first time, did she dream about glorious sermons, victorious parades, and adoring crowds? Or did she have an idea that Jesus' life would not follow the path most people expected?

Whether or not she had an inkling about His unusual ministry, it must have been difficult to watch Him grow up "different" from other children. Though He astounded scholars in the temple at the age of twelve, He returned home to learn a simple trade with His father. And He didn't start His earthly ministry until He turned thirty. During those years, did she wonder about God's plans? I bet she got very comfortable having Him around, and enjoyed His company—His great mind, His kind heart, the way He honored her and Joseph with everything He did—immensely.

When He began to preach and teach, Jesus seemed to almost reject her and their family. The pain must have been intense for Mary. All His life, she had nurtured, protected, and defended Him to His friends and family. And now He was stating that His *real* family members were the people who obeyed God.

And then she heard that the crowd turned on Him and nearly killed Him when He read publicly from Isaiah! Did she wonder if He had lost his mind? Did her thoughts wander back to the day when Simeon had prophesied that a "sword would pierce her soul"?

Motherhood is tough. On the good days, it's wonderful. And on the bad days, it's horrible. When our child says, "I hate you!" or tells us that he can't wait to leave home, our hearts ache. When other kids reject our son or daughter, and we see them in pain, we feel the hurt and grieve with him. When they begin to make noises about leaving us—perhaps even following a dream or a call that will take them far away—we panic.

Some of us moms deal with those kinds of situations by becoming overprotective. Trying to control our kids' futures, we attempt to keep our kids safe and limit their pain. But when we try too hard to avoid heartache, either theirs or ours, we end up shortchanging them.

Our culture tends to overemphasize safety and security, to the detriment of a risky faith. But Jesus calls us to be countercultural. He wants us to set an example of obeying Him, even when it's hard. And when our children follow in our footsteps, we need to take a deep breath, pray over them, and let them do what He's calling them to do. It's not easy, but God will reward our obedience—and theirs.

Ask God to help you allow your kids to follow hard after God, no matter the cost to you or them. It's scary, but God promises to help.

Think It Over

• How do you try to keep your kids safe?

• In what ways do you identify with Mary, the mother of Jesus?

• How could you encourage your children to follow hard after God?

I know the LORD is always with me.
I will not be shaken, for he is right beside me.
PSALM 16:8 NLT

A Sympathetic Friend
Naomi
Ruth 1 NLV

In the days when there were judges to rule, there was a time of no food in the land. A certain man of Bethlehem in Judah went to visit the land of Moab with his wife and his two sons. The name of the man was Elimelech. His wife's name was Naomi. And the names of his two sons were Mahlon and Chilion. They were Ephrathites of Bethlehem in Judah. They went into the land of Moab and stayed there. But Naomi's husband Elimelech died. And she was left with her two sons, who married Moabite women. The name of one was Orpah. The name of the other was Ruth. After living there about ten years, both Mahlon and Chilion died. Naomi was left without her two children and her husband.

Then Naomi got ready to return from the land of Moab with her daughters-in-law. She had heard in the land of Moab that the Lord had brought food to His people. So she left with her two daughters-in-law and went on the way toward the land of Judah. But Naomi said to her two daughters-in-law, "Go, each one of you return to your own mother's house. May the Lord show kindness to you, as you have done with the dead and with me. May the Lord help you to find a home, each in the family of her husband." Then she kissed them, and they cried in loud voices. They said to her, "No, we will return with you to your people."

But Naomi said, "Return to your people, my daughters. Why should you go with me? Do I have more sons within me, who could become your husbands? Return, my daughters. Go. For I am too old to have a husband. If I had hope, if I should have a husband tonight and give birth to sons, would you wait until they were grown? Would you not marry until then? No, my daughters. It is harder for me than for you. For the hand of the Lord is against me."

Then they cried again in loud voices. Orpah kissed her mother-in-law. But Ruth held on to her.

Naomi said, "See, your sister-in-law has returned to her people and her gods. Return after your sister-in-law."

But Ruth said, "Do not beg me to leave you or turn away from following you. I will go where you go. I will live where you live. Your people will be my people. And your God will be my God. I will die where you die, and there I will be buried. So may the Lord do the same to me, and worse, if anything but death takes me from you."

When Naomi saw that Ruth would do nothing but go with her, she said no more to her.

So they both went until they came to Bethlehem. The whole town of Bethlehem was happy because of them. The women said, "Is this Naomi?"

She said to them, "Do not call me Naomi. Call me Mara. For the All-powerful has brought much trouble to me. I went out full. But the Lord has made me return empty. Why call me Naomi? The Lord has spoken against me. The All-powerful has allowed me to suffer."

So Naomi returned. And her daughter-in-law Ruth, the Moabite woman, returned with her from the land of Moab. They came to Bethlehem at the beginning of barley gathering time.

A Sympathetic Friend
Naomi
Life Application

Naomi must have been a remarkable woman. After all, she inspired her widowed daughter-in-law to stay by her side indefinitely.

The two women came from different countries and had little in common, yet their relationship overcame their dissimilarities. Perhaps they shared hopes and dreams as they cooked meals for their husbands. Maybe Naomi told Ruth stories about her homeland as she wistfully looked out over the horizon. Though the country suffered from a famine, Naomi certainly missed her home, friends, and town.

When life crashed in around Ruth and Naomi, suddenly they had the label "widow" in common. Tears flowed as they discussed their few prospects as single women. And though Naomi longed for home, she had been gone ten years. Fear gripped her heart as she contemplated the long journey alone. But unselfishly, she insisted that her daughters-in-law return to their own people, where they would be more likely to remarry.

Ruth couldn't be deterred, however. By this time, her affection for Naomi ran deep, and she determined to follow her mother-in-love wherever she went. Together, they faced the crowds who gathered as they entered Bethlehem. Together, they told Naomi's friends and kin the tragedies they had experienced in Moab.

Though Naomi's name meant "pleasant," she insisted that her townspeople now call her "bitter." Naomi declared: "God has left me with nothing."

But she was wrong. He gave her Ruth, who would eventually give her a grandson. And that grandson, Obed, became an ancestor to Jesus.

❧

When we suffer excruciating losses, it's easy for us to lose hope. Sometimes we can barely move. When friends and family try to comfort us, we push them away. Even our faith in God seems like a cruel hoax. "You've left me with nothing!" we rail at Him.

Yet, even when we attempt to reject Him, God in His mercy doesn't reject us. And He sends other people to encourage us in our sorrow.

Moms who endure miscarriage or stillbirth deal with terrible pain, both physically and emotionally. Many of them fall into deep depression, and because their kind of loss isn't often talked about, their grief can last for years. Since most pregnancy losses don't necessitate a funeral service, a lack of closure exacerbates the problem.

But miscarriage and stillbirth are real losses, and fellow moms can reach out to help those who suffer from each. Have you been through this type of death? Try and share your story when it's appropriate, in order to help others understand your pain. Do you know a mom who has lost a child? Take her a meal or give some kind of memorial to acknowledge that her loss was real.

Today, if you're in Naomi's situation, take hope. And if you're in Ruth's shoes, reach out.

Think It Over

•   How do you relate to Naomi?

•   What things tempt you to become bitter?

•   Who around you is suffering?

•   If so, how could you be an encouragement
    to them?

*The LORD is close to the brokenhearted and
saves those who are crushed in spirit.*
PSALM 34:18 NIV

God as Our Security
Noah's Wife
Abridged from Genesis 6 NLV

The Lord saw that man was very sinful on the earth. Every plan and thought of the heart of man was sinful always. The Lord was sorry that He had made man on the earth. He had sorrow in His heart. So the Lord said, "I will destroy man whom I have made from the land, man and animals, things that move upon the earth and birds of the sky. For I am sorry that I have made them." But Noah found favor in the eyes of the Lord.

This is the story of Noah and his family. Noah was right with God. He was without blame in his time. Noah walked with God. And Noah became the father of three sons: Shem, Ham, and Japheth.

Now the earth was sinful in the eyes of God. The earth was filled with people hurting each other. God looked at the earth and saw how sinful it was. For all who lived on the earth had become sinful in their ways.

Then God said to Noah, "I have decided to make an end to all the people on the earth. They are the cause of very much trouble. See, I will destroy them as I destroy the earth. Make a large boat of gopher wood for yourself. Build rooms in the boat. And cover it inside and out with tar. This is how you are to make it: The boat is to be as long as 150 long steps, as wide as twenty-five long steps, and eight times taller than a man. Make a window for the boat, that goes down an arm's length from the roof. Put a door in the side of the boat. And make it with first, second, and third floors. See, I will bring a flood of water upon the earth, to destroy all flesh under heaven that has the breath of life. Everything on earth will be destroyed.

"But I will make My agreement with you. You will go into the large boat, you and your sons and your wife, and your sons' wives with you. You are to bring into the large boat two of every kind of living thing of all flesh, to keep them alive with you. They will be male and female. Two of all the kinds of birds, and animals, and every thing that moves on the ground are to be with you to keep them alive. And take with you every kind of food that is eaten, and store it. It will be food for you and for them."

Noah did just what God told him to do.

God as Our Security
Noah's Wife
Life Application

Even before God told Noah to construct the ark, his family must have been quite lonely. The scriptures note that Noah was a righteous man, blameless among the people of his time. As someone who walked with God in the midst of a corrupt generation, Noah probably didn't have many close friends. Most likely, he and his kin were misunderstood and mistreated. So even before their long boat trip, the family's secluded lifestyle had forged lasting bonds between the members of Noah's brood.

As the mistress of the clan, Noah's wife is barely mentioned in this passage—but she had an unmistakable role in God's plan. Without his wife's support, Noah probably would have disobeyed God's instructions. After all, a huge job like ark-building could find real success only if the builder had his spouse cheering him on.

Still, Noah's wife must have had tons of questions: "God told you *what*?" "What do you mean you're supposed to take animals with you?" "Just what are we supposed to feed them?"

At night, did she toss and turn as she pictured the coming destruction? Did she wonder if her husband had indeed heard from God—or if he was just crazy?

Whatever her initial reaction, she eventually left her home and everything familiar to board a huge boat when there wasn't even a drop of rain. Her heart ached as the crowds laughed and jeered, throwing stones at the man she loved. . .and her sons.

Sometimes today's moms—especially those whose husbands walk passionately with God—are asked to do crazy things. One woman's spouse comes home from a Bible study with a new revelation from the Lord—which will mean a huge lifestyle change. Another's husband admits he's heard a call to ministry, which will probably lead to seminary, financial hardship, and relocation.

A mom whose husband left a job with benefits for a precarious position with an underfunded nonprofit organization said she struggled with fear the first few months of the job, but she eventually learned how to trust God for their monthly finances. Every single time a bill came due, money eventually came in so they could pay it—on time.

Another mom's teenage children encouraged their parents to adopt an orphan child, even though the couple was looking forward to a soon-to-be empty nest. Now, three adopted kids later, the family can't imagine life without their children from across the world. It hasn't been an easy ride for them, but their joy and peace radiates. They are a family who've learned to trust God's leadership, though at times His plan can seem crazy.

What about you? Are you willing to say "yes" to even the most unlikely requests from your heavenly Father? When you do, He'll reward you.

Think It Over

- When have you seen God ask one of His followers to do something "crazy"?

- Have you ever taken a leap of faith? If not, why not?

- If so, what was the outcome?

- What things make you feel secure? Could you give them up if God asked you to?

I know, O LORD, that a man's life is not his own; it is not for man to direct his steps.
JEREMIAH 10:23 NIV

The Strength to Forgive
Peninnah

Abridged from I Samuel I NLV

There was a certain man from Ramathaim-zophim of the hill country of Ephraim. His name was Elkanah, the son of Jeroham, the son of Elihu, the son of Tohu, the son of Zuph, an Ephraimite. He had two wives. The name of one was Hannah. The name of the other was Peninnah. Peninnah had children, but Hannah had no children.

This man would go from his city each year to worship and to give gifts on the altar in Shiloh to the Lord of All. Eli's two sons, Hophni and Phinehas, were the Lord's religious leaders there. On the day when Elkanah killed animals on the altar in worship, he would give part of the gift to his wife Peninnah and to all her sons and daughters. But he would give twice as much to Hannah, for he loved Hannah. But the Lord had made it so she could not have children. Peninnah would try to make her very angry, because the Lord would not let her have children.

So it happened, year after year, each time Hannah went up to the house of the Lord, Peninnah would make her angry. Hannah cried and would not eat.

Then her husband Elkanah said to her, "Hannah, why are you crying? Why are you not eating, and why is your heart sad? Am I not better to you than ten sons?"

The Strength to Forgive
Peninnah
Life Application

Peninnah finally sat down at the dinner table after corralling her kids inside for the evening meal. Peninnah looked over at Hannah, who was already halfway through her meal. "So, Hannah," she said, "you'll be done eating before me. Why don't you do all the dishes tonight? You have so much time on your hands anyway, since you don't have any children."

Hannah ignored Peninnah and cut her meat slowly. "I'd be glad to do the dishes," she said. "And don't worry about me—I have plenty to keep me busy."

"Oh, yes, I forgot," Peninnah said. "You're knitting all the clothes for the babies you'll never have." She smiled, but it didn't reach her eyes.

Suddenly, Hannah put down her utensils. She held back a sob with a hand to her mouth as tears sprang to her eyes. She pushed back from the table and ran out of the room.

Elkanah sat down, exasperated that Peninnah had insulted his other wife again. But he knew Hannah well enough that he didn't follow her. This scene had repeated itself one too many times, with Hannah always insisting she be left alone to recover.

"What do you think you're doing? Don't you think Hannah suffers enough, without your cruel input?"

Peninnah, a haughty and arrogant woman, seemed to enjoy taunting Hannah. Perhaps she was jealous of the gentle, thoughtful way her husband treated his other wife. Maybe she was short-tempered because of lack of sleep (she did have several children, after all!). But whatever her motives, Peninnah relentlessly threw poisoned barbs at Hannah.

However, even though Peninnah daily flaunted her fertility in Hannah's presence, Hannah refused to strike back. Instead, she brought her wounded heart and unanswered prayers to the Lord. What a great role model for modern women!

Moms, how do we react when someone mistreats us? Do we gossip behind her back? Ask God to strike her down? Or just think mean thoughts in her general direction?

Hannah knew that gossip, nasty thoughts, and vengeful requests weren't effective in the long run. Because she had spent so much time in prayer, she had a sense that God would take care of her enemies. Perhaps God's spirit had given her a glimpse of Peninnah's empty heart, causing Hannah to have compassion on her shameless rival.

The saying "hurting people hurt people" seems fitting here. When people wound us, we should leave their punishment to the Lord, praying for them to find healing in Him. While we're at it, we can pray that God will hold us in His arms, heal our hearts, and give us the strength to forgive.

And He has promised to do just that.

Think It Over

- What was the last time someone hurt you deeply?

- How did you handle the situation?

- Today, say a prayer for that person. Ask God for the will to forgive them, if you haven't.

"Here's another old saying that deserves a second look: 'Eye for eye, tooth for tooth.' Is that going to get us anywhere? Here's what I propose: 'Don't hit back at all.' If someone strikes you, stand there and take it. If someone drags you into court and sues for the shirt off your back, gift-wrap your best coat and make a present of it. And if someone takes unfair advantage of you, use the occasion to practice the servant life. No more tit-for-tat stuff. Live generously."
MATTHEW 5:38–42 MSG

The Call to Adopt
Pharaoh's Daughter

Abridged from Exodus 1–2 NLV

The king of Egypt spoke to the Hebrew nurses. The name of one was Shiphrah. The name of the other was Puah. He said, "When you are helping the Hebrew women to give birth, and see the baby before the mother does, if it is a son, kill him. But if it is a daughter, let her live."

But the nurses feared God. They did not do what the king of Egypt told them. They let the boys live.

So the king of Egypt called the nurses and said to them, "Why have you done this, and let the boys live?"

The nurses answered Pharaoh, "Because the Hebrew women are not like the Egyptian women. They are strong. They give birth before the nurse comes to them."

So God was good to the nurses. And the people became many and strong. Because the nurses feared God, He gave them families.

Then Pharaoh told all his people, "Throw every son who is born to the Hebrews into the Nile. But keep every daughter alive."

Now a man of the family of Levi married a daughter of Levi. She was going to have a baby, and she gave birth to a son. When she saw that he was beautiful, she hid him for three months.

But the time came when she could hide him no longer. So she took a basket made from grass, and covered it with tar and put the child in it. And she set it in the grass by the side of the Nile. His sister stayed to watch and find out what would happen to him.

Then the daughter of Pharaoh came to wash herself in the Nile. Her young women walked beside the Nile. She saw the basket in the tall grass and sent the woman who served her to get it.

She opened it and saw the child. The boy was crying. She had pity on him and said, "This is one of the Hebrews' children."

Then his sister said to Pharaoh's daughter, "Should I go and call a nurse from the Hebrew women to nurse the child for you?"

Pharaoh's daughter said to her, "Go." So the girl went and called the child's mother. Then Pharaoh's daughter said to her, "Take this child away and nurse him for me. And I will pay you."

So the woman took the child and nursed him. The child grew, and she brought him to Pharaoh's daughter. And he became her son. She gave him the name Moses, saying, "Because I took him out of the water."

The Call to Adopt
Pharaoh's Daughter
Life Application

The story of Moses' first few months is filled with courageous women. And God used each of them in different ways to protect and prepare the man who would someday lead His people out of slavery.

Pharaoh saw the Hebrews growing in number and strength, so he instructed the midwives to kill every Hebrew boy child. But because the midwives feared God more than their earthly ruler, they disobeyed his command. That act led to Pharaoh issuing yet another cruel edict: All Hebrew boy babies must be drowned.

When Moses was born, his mother saw something special in him. At the risk of her own life, she devised a brave plan to hide him, and when he grew too big, she placed him in a basket and put him in the river. "Protect him, Lord," she prayed, and she sent her daughter to look after the baby.

In God's providence, Pharaoh's daughter was bathing along the Nile with her servants, and she found the basket. She recognized the baby as Hebrew, but her heart warmed to the child, and she protected him instead of following her father's orders. And when Moses' sister offered to find a nurse for the baby, she readily agreed. Later, she adopted Moses and raised him as her son.

The story of Pharaoh's daughter brings to mind several points about adoption. First, it's a calling. Tina, an adoptive mom who also has biological children, says, "It's not a second-best option. It's not a cure for a couple that's unable to have children. It is a call! Just as we are called to a certain job or ministry, the Lord calls just the right people to adopt a child."

Second, it takes courage. Some people think adopting is an easy way to have kids. But it can be a long, hard, emotional process. Tina and her husband had two possibilities fall through during the process of adopting their daughter. Both were heart wrenching and devastating. With help from her husband and a colleague, Tina was able to work through those struggles, but it was not an easy time for her.

Third, it's a picture of what God has done for us. As Christians we are *all* adopted. None of us is a biological child of God. Through the cross, He has grafted us into His family tree.

When a friend is considering adoption, be sensitive with the things you say about the subject. Try not to say, "Why don't you 'just' adopt?" because that makes the process seem as simple as going to the grocery store for a loaf of bread. Please don't ask a family whose children look different from them, "Are they yours?" because adoptive parents consider every child "theirs," whether they are their biological children or not.

And don't forget: You were adopted, too. Your name is engraved in the Book of Life, and God is your adoptive father. Now *that's* something to celebrate!

- What courageous choices have you made in raising your children?

- How has God honored those decisions?

- Which point about adoption do you think is the most important?

- How does knowing you're adopted by God make you feel?

For he chose us in him before the creation of the world to be holy and blameless in his sight. In love he predestined us to be adopted as his sons through Jesus Christ, in accordance with his pleasure and will—to the praise of his glorious grace, which he has freely given us in the One he loves.
EPHESIANS 1:4–6 NIV

The Agony of Infertility
Rachel (Part 1)

Abridged from Genesis 30, 35 NLV

When Rachel saw that she had not given birth to any children for Jacob, she became jealous of her sister. She said to Jacob, "Give me children, or else I am going to die!"

Then Jacob became angry with Rachel. He said, "Am I taking God's place, Who has kept you from giving birth?"

Then she said, "Here is Bilhah, the woman who serves me. Go in to her, and let her give birth for me. Even I may have children through her." So she gave Bilhah to him for a wife, the woman who served her. And Jacob went in to her. Bilhah was going to have a child and she gave birth to a son.

Then Rachel said, "God has done the right thing for me. He has heard my voice and has given me a son." So she gave him the name Dan. Bilhah. . .was going to have another child. And she gave birth to another son for Jacob. So Rachel said, "I have fought a hard fight with my sister, and I have won." She gave him the name Naphtali. . . .

Then God remembered Rachel. God listened to her, and made her able to have a child, and she gave birth to a son. Then she said, "God has taken away my shame." She gave him the name Joseph, saying, "May the Lord give me another son. . . ."

Then they traveled from Bethel. When there was still a long way to go before coming to Ephrath, Rachel began to give birth. She suffered much pain. And while she was suffering, the woman who was helping her said to her, "Do not be afraid. For now you have another son."

As Rachel's soul was leaving, for she died, she gave him the name Benoni. But his father gave him the name Benjamin. So Rachel died, and was buried on the way to Ephrath (that is, Bethlehem). Jacob set up a stone on her grave. And that is the stone of Rachel's grave to this day.

The Agony of Infertility
Rachel (Part 1)
Life Application

Jacob married two wives and had two concubines. The concubines were referred to as Leah's and Rachel's maidservants, but by ancient law, they could have Jacob's children at the bidding of his wives, and the children could then be adopted by Leah and Rachel. Rachel was Jacob's favorite wife and was often given preferential treatment, but Leah was fertile and could have Jacob's children without the help of a maidservant.

In frustration, Rachel gave her maidservant, Bilhah, to Jacob. Jacob slept with Bilhah and she bore him two sons, whom Rachel adopted. When she named the two boys, she gave them names which meant "I have wrestled with my sister and overcome" and "the Lord has vindicated me." It's ironic that Rachel felt that she was in a battle with Leah; after all, Jacob never really loved Leah. But a woman's ability to bear her own children—especially male heirs—was seen as the ultimate reward, and Rachel would never be satisfied until she had children of her own. Ultimately, she herself conceived two sons with Jacob—Joseph, who became Jacob's favorite son, and Benjamin. In a sad turn of events, Rachel died after giving birth to Benjamin.

Women who have a difficult—or impossible—time conceiving a child can relate to Rachel. The longing to have a baby can seem overwhelming. At times, it can even override a woman's better judgment. Infertile women deal with guilt, doubt, and depression. Their monthly cycle seems to mock them, and sends them on a roller-coaster ride of hope and despair. Some families spend thousands of dollars on infertility tests and treatment. And often, the treatments don't work—which leads to more questions and frustration.

Women who can't conceive are often tempted to envy those who are blessed with fertility. "What have they got that I haven't?" they sometimes ask. "Is God punishing me or my husband?" Other people often do harm with their careless or thoughtless words by saying things like, "At least you have your husband," or "Why don't you trust God?" When a couple is struggling to conceive a second child, people often carelessly suggest, "Be happy with the child you have."

If you struggle with infertility, know that God is a loving Father who longs to hold you. He can give you the peace your heart desires. And know also that people will sometimes say terrible things—but usually because they don't know any better. Whether or not we're hurt, we have a choice in how we react.

So take your sorrow to Him, and let Him wrap His arms around you. He can save, comfort, and lift your spirit.

Think It Over

- How has infertility had an impact on your life or those close to you?

- What are some of the emotions you've felt?

- How can you encourage others who are dealing with this issue?

- Have you given your own struggles—in this or any area of your life—to God? If not, why not?

*He will swallow up death forever,
and the Lord GOD will wipe away tears from all
faces; the rebuke of His people He will take away
from all the earth; for the LORD has spoken.*
ISAIAH 25:8 NKJV

The Sin of Jealousy
Rachel (Part 2)
Abridged from Genesis 29 NLV

Then Jacob went on his way and came to the land of the people of the east. He looked up and saw a well in the field where three flocks of sheep were lying beside it. The people gave water to the flocks from that well. The stone covering the top of the well was large. When all the flocks were gathered there, the men would roll the stone from the top of the well. Then after giving water to the sheep, they would put the stone again in its place on top of the well.

Jacob said to them, "My brothers, where are you from?"

They said, "We are from Haran."

He said to them, "Do you know Laban the son of Nahor?"

They said, "We know him."

He asked them, "Is he well?"

They said, "He is well. And see, his daughter Rachel is coming with the sheep."

Jacob said, "See, the sun is still high. It is not time for the flocks to be gathered. Give water to the sheep, and return them to their field."

But they said, "We cannot, until all the flocks are gathered and they roll the stone from the top of the well. Then we will give the sheep water."

He was still talking with them when Rachel came with her father's sheep, for she cared for them. When Jacob saw Rachel the daughter of his mother's brother

Laban, and the sheep of his mother's brother Laban, Jacob went near and rolled the stone from the top of the well. And he gave water to the flock of his mother's brother Laban. Then Jacob kissed Rachel and began to cry for joy. Jacob told Rachel that he was of her father's family, the son of Rebekah. And she ran and told her father.

When Laban heard the news of his sister's son Jacob, he ran to meet him. He put his arms around him and kissed him, and brought him to his house. Then Jacob told Laban all these things. Laban said to him, "For sure you are my bone and my flesh." And Jacob stayed with him a month.

The Sin of Jealousy
Rachel (Part 2)
Life Application

Jacob, helped by his mother, deceived his father and took the blessing that he coveted—a blessing that rightfully belonged to his older brother, Esau. Later, after moving away to distance himself from Esau's wrath, Jacob fell desperately in love with Rachel—at first sight. In fact, his desire for her was so strong that he worked seven years to marry her. Then he worked seven more years when his father-in-law deceived him and sent Leah to the marriage bed on Jacob and Rachel's wedding night. What a mess!

And though Leah bore him several sons, Jacob never loved Leah, always preferring her sister, Rachel. Almost certainly, Leah was jealous of Rachel's beauty and the hold she had on Jacob—but Rachel was envious of her sister's ability to bear her own children.

The entire story of Jacob and Rachel is filled with missteps and bad decisions. Many of those probably originated with the emotional baggage they all carried, stemming from a family pattern of deception, jealousy, and sibling rivalry. And yet God blessed Jacob with twelve sons, who would become the twelve tribes of Israel. Through all their foibles and failings, God never gave up on the family of Jacob. That fact can comfort us as moms.

❧

Julie spent many of her adolescent years jealous of her older sister. Jill seemed to have it all—looks, brains, popularity, and boys galore. Julie, on the other hand, struggled in relationships and with her schoolwork. Success and happiness didn't come easily for her. In high school, things began to turn around for her when she accepted Christ as her Savior at a youth camp. He slowly and lovingly filled the holes in her soul. He became her confidante, her best friend, and her confidence.

Years later, however, she still struggled with jealousy—especially of her sister. Jill had a husband whose job provided them with countless material blessings, and Jill was able to stay home with her kids. She and her husband had a great house, a thriving business, and a loving relationship. Their kids were adorable and smart, and they went to private school.

Julie's life wasn't that successful on the outside. She needed to work because her husband was in a fulfilling but low-paying ministry position. Their car was old, their carpets threadbare, and their savings nonexistent. One day, during her time with God, Julie sighed. "I'm tired of being jealous." And then she heard something that surprised her—an answer. "I'm tired of it, too!" God spoke to her heart.

Julie repented and asked God for His strength to overcome the sin of jealousy. As she confessed, her heart felt light and free. She even prayed for God to bless her sister *more*.

Think It Over

* In what situations do you struggle with jealousy?

* Do you have brothers and sisters? How is your relationship?

* How can the story of Rachel and Jacob give us hope as moms?

*The acts of the sinful nature are obvious:
sexual immorality, impurity and debauchery;
idolatry and witchcraft; hatred, discord, jealousy,
fits of rage, selfish ambition, dissensions, factions and
envy; drunkenness, orgies, and the like. I warn you,
as I did before, that those who live like this will
not inherit the kingdom of God.*
GALATIANS 5:19–21 NIV

Desperate to Secure a Blessing
Rebekah

Abridged from Genesis 25–27 NLV

Isaac prayed to the Lord for his wife, because she could not give birth and the Lord answered him. Rebekah was able to give birth.

But the babies within her fought together. And she said, "If this is so, why am I like this?" She went to ask the Lord why.

The Lord said to her, "Two nations are within you. Two peoples will be divided from your body. One will be stronger than the other. And the older will serve the younger."

When the day came for her to give birth, there were two babies to be born. . . . When the boys grew older, Esau became a good hunter, a man of the field. But Jacob was a man of peace, living in tents. Isaac showed favor to Esau, because he liked to eat the meat of the animals Esau killed. But Rebekah showed favor to Jacob. . . .

Isaac was now old, and had become blind. He called to his older son Esau, saying, "My son."

And Esau answered, "Here I am."

Isaac said, "See, I am old. I do not know when I will die. Take your bow and arrows, and go out to the field to get meat for me. Get some food ready for me that I love. Bring it to me to eat, so that before I die I will pray that good will come to you."

And Rebekah was listening while Isaac spoke to his son Esau. So when Esau went to the field to hunt for meat to bring home, Rebekah said to her son Jacob,

". . . Go to the flock and bring me two fat young goats. I will cook them into good-tasting food, just what your father loves to eat. Then you will take it to your father for him to eat. So before he dies he will pray for good to come to you. . . ."

So Jacob went and got them, and brought them to his mother. And his mother made good-tasting food, just what his father loved to eat. Then Rebekah took the best clothes that belonged to her older son Esau, that were with her in the house. And she put them on her younger son Jacob. She put the skins of the young goats on his hands and on the smooth part of his neck. And she gave her son Jacob the bread and the good-tasting food she had made.

Then he went to his father and said, "My father."

Isaac said, "Here I am. Who are you, my son?"

Jacob said to his father, "I am Esau, your first-born. I have done as you told me. Sit up and eat the meat I brought, so you will pray that good will come to me. . . ."

Then Isaac said to Jacob, "Come near so I can touch you, my son, to know for sure if you are my son Esau or not."

So Jacob came near his father Isaac. Isaac touched him, and said, "The voice is Jacob's voice. But the hands are Esau's hands." He did not know who he was, because his hands were covered with hair like his brother Esau's hands. So Isaac prayed that good would come to him.

Desperate to Secure a Blessing
Rebekah
Life Application

Like many moms, Rebekah believed she knew what was best for her children—especially her favorite son, Jacob. God had promised that Esau would serve Jacob, and she wanted to help God out and move the prophecy along. She became greedy for her husband's blessing for her youngest.

So Rebekah, who had seen God move mightily before (she was barren before God opened her womb and gave her twins), and who should have trusted Him to fulfill His word in His timing, created a plan to deceive Isaac. Rebekah believed that Jacob deserved the blessing, allowing her love for Jacob to overshadow her faith in God's providence.

In fact, she allowed her emotions to override everything else, including the fact that she would have to lie and cheat to steal a blessing. For her, the end really did justify the means. Like Sarah, who gave Abraham her servant Hagar to sleep with, Rebekah felt like she could do a better job of making things happen than God.

But don't be too quick to judge Rebekah. After all, we often do the same thing. We forget that God is in charge of our kids' lives, and we let our emotions overtake our common sense. If we're not prayerful, we can try to manipulate situations in order to secure "blessings" for our children.

We look at other parents and wonder if we're doing enough. Their children are in this club and on that honor roll, and we worry that our kids will fall behind if they're not doing and achieving the same things. We want our children to succeed, and we become greedy.

Perhaps we choose our kids' school without praying about it because of its rigorous academic challenges, knowing that they might struggle there. But we justify the expense (and our children's misery) by saying, "It will look good on your college application!"

Or maybe we push them into a sport with a high injury rate—cheerleading, football, or gymnastics—because we long for them to be the next gold medal or Heisman trophy winner. But what if they aren't athletically gifted and don't even want to be involved in sports?

For whatever reason—a lack of approval in our own childhood, too much ambition, or simply wanting our child to be happy—moms can take the steering wheel and drive our kids right over the cliff.

The only way to be sure we're letting our kids follow the path God designed for them is to pray our way through decisions. God will give us wisdom and discernment. Then we can guide our children in the way they're meant to go.

Think It Over

- Do you relate to Rebekah? Why?

- How have you tried to make things happen for your kids instead of letting God lead?

- How did that turn out?

- In what areas of your kids' lives do you need to lower your expectations and let God take control?

Let nothing be done through selfish ambition or conceit, but in lowliness of mind let each esteem others better than himself. Let each of you look out not only for his own interests, but also for the interests of others.
PHILIPPIANS 2:3–4 NKJV

The Gift of a Faithful Friend
Ruth

Abridged from the book of Ruth NLV

Naomi said [to Ruth], "See, your sister-in-law has returned to her people and her gods. Return after your sister-in-law."

But Ruth said, "Do not beg me to leave you or turn away from following you. I will go where you go. I will live where you live. Your people will be my people. And your God will be my God. I will die where you die, and there I will be buried. So may the Lord do the same to me, and worse, if anything but death takes me from you."

When Naomi saw that Ruth would do nothing but go with her, she said no more to her. . . .

There was an in-law of the family of Naomi's husband there whose name was Boaz. He was a very rich man of the family of Elimelech. Ruth, the Moabite woman, said to Naomi, "Let me go to the field to gather grain behind someone who might show favor to me." Naomi said to her, "Go, my daughter." So Ruth went and gathered in the field behind those who picked the grain. And she happened to come to the part of the field that belonged to Boaz, who was of the family of Elimelech. . . .

Then Boaz said to his servant who was watching over those who gathered grain, "Whose young woman is this?"

The servant who watched over those who gathered grain said, "She is the young Moabite woman who returned with Naomi from the land of Moab. . . ."

Then Boaz said to Ruth, "Be careful to listen, my daughter. Do not go to gather grain in another field. Do not leave this one. But stay here with my women who gather grain. Keep your eyes upon the field where they gather grain. Go behind them. I have told the servants not to touch you. When you are thirsty, go to the water jars. Drink the water the servants have put there."

Then she fell with her face to the ground and said to him, "Why have I found favor in your eyes? Why do you care about me? I am a stranger from another land."

Boaz said to her, "I have heard about all you have done for your mother-in-law after the death of your husband. I have heard how you left your father and mother and the land of your birth to come to a people you did not know before. May the Lord reward you for your work. May full pay be given to you from the Lord, the God of Israel. It is under His wings that you have come to be safe. . . ."

So Boaz took Ruth. She became his wife, and he went in to her. The Lord made it possible for her to have a child and she gave birth to a son. The women said to Naomi, "Thanks be to the Lord. He has not left you without a family this day. May his name become known in all of Israel. May he bring you new life and strength while you are old. For your daughter-in-law who loves you, who is better to you than seven sons, has given birth to him."

Then Naomi took the child and held him, and became his nurse. The neighbor women gave him a name. They said, "A son has been born to Naomi!" And they called him Obed. He is the father of Jesse, the father of David.

The Gift of a Faithful Friend
Ruth
Life Application

No one would have blamed Ruth if she'd done what Orpah did and left Naomi. Everyone would have understood if she'd traveled back to her own country and people. After all, as a young childless widow, she had no hope of providing for herself. She needed to find a husband, or she would end up destitute.

But with a pure heart full of love, Ruth refused to leave her mother-in-law—her friend—alone. Instead, she set out with her and joined their fates together. Wherever Naomi decided to live, Ruth promised to stay by her side. And she vowed to do so until one of them died.

Ruth's statement to Naomi has reverberated through centuries and has been used in countless wedding ceremonies. Its power and beauty lies in its unwavering commitment and unconditional love.

Forget mother-in-law jokes—Ruth was an exemplary friend to her husband's mother. The story of what she did for Naomi traveled far, and people she had never met admired her.

Boaz heard of Ruth's selflessness and gave her his favor. What man wouldn't want such a devoted wife? After all, marriage is not much of a relationship without friendship as a basis. Eventually, Boaz and Ruth married and had a son, who was an ancestor of David and of Jesus. A new family—and a grandson for Naomi— became Ruth's reward for her faithfulness.

Faithful friends like Ruth are hard to find, but they're priceless. Friends enrich our lives with lunches, notes, road trips, hugs, and conversation. God can use them as counselors, cheerleaders, and even coaches—to encourage us when we're down, support us when we're stressed, rejoice with us when we're feeling triumphant, and even bring us down a few notches when we deserve it.

But being a mother means our time to cultivate and nurture friendships is limited. So what's a busy mom to do? Well, first of all, we can pray for friends—knowing that God planted the desire for community in our hearts. He will be faithful to provide the friends we need in the different seasons of our lives. And mothering is a season where friendship is not just beneficial—it's essential.

Second, we can be friendly as we're going about our daily lives. Do you work out? Look for friends in your aerobics class or in the weight room. If your child is enrolled in a class or school, search for like-minded moms at parents' events. Does your church host a moms' group? Go, at least once, and give it a chance—even if you're shy. Start conversations, ask questions, and listen.

Finally, be open to God's surprises. God may select someone to be your friend that you'd never pick, but He knows us better than we know ourselves. So often, we gravitate toward people who are just like us, and we miss opportunities to learn from people who are different from us.

Think It Over

- What qualities are essential to you in a friend?

- What does friendship mean to you?

- How can you open yourself to God's relational surprises?

- How can you be a better friend?

> *A friend loves at all times,*
> *and a brother is born for adversity.*
> PROVERBS 17:17 NIV

When God Does the Impossible
Sarah (Part 1)

Abridged from Genesis 15, 17, 21 NLV

After these things, the word of the Lord came to Abram in a special dream, saying, "Do not be afraid, Abram. I am your safe place. Your reward will be very great."

Then Abram said, "O Lord God, what will You give me? For I have no child. And the one who is to receive what belongs to me is Eliezer of Damascus." Abram said, "Because You have not given me a child, one born in my house will be given all I have."

Then the word of the Lord came to him, saying, "This man will not be given what is yours. But he who will come from your own body will be given what is yours." He took him outside and said, "Now look up into the heavens and add up the stars, if you are able to number them." Then He said to him, "Your children and your children's children will be as many as the stars."

Then Abram believed in the Lord, and that made him right with God. . . .

When Abram was ninety-nine years old, the Lord came to him and said, "I am God All-powerful. Obey Me, and be without blame. And I will keep My agreement between Me and you. I will give you many children."

Then Abram fell on his face. God said to him, "See, My agreement is with you. You will be the father of many nations. No more will your name be Abram. But your name will be Abraham. For I will make you the father of many nations. Many will come from you. I will make nations of you. Kings will come from you. I will make My agreement between Me and you and your children after you through their whole lives for all time. I will be God to you and to your children's children after you. I will give to you and your children after you the land in which you are a stranger, all the land of Canaan for yourselves forever. And I will be their God. . . ."

Then God said to Abraham, "As for Sarai your wife, do not call her name Sarai. But Sarah will be her name. And I will bring good to her. I will give you a son by her. I will bring good to her. And she will be the mother of nations. Kings of many people will come from her."

Then Abraham fell on his face and laughed. He said to himself, "Will a child be born to a man who is 100 years old? . . ."

But God said, "No, but your wife Sarah will give birth to your son. And you will give him the name Isaac. I will make My agreement with him and for his children after him, an agreement that will last forever. . . ."

When He had finished talking with him, God went up from Abraham. . . .

Then the Lord visited Sarah as He had said and did for her as He had promised. Sarah was able to have a child and she gave birth to a son when Abraham was very old. He was born at the time the Lord said it would happen. . . . Abraham was one hundred years old when Isaac was born. And Sarah said, "God has made me laugh. All who hear will laugh with me." She said, "Who would have said to Abraham that Sarah would nurse children? Yet when he is so old I have given him a son."

When God Does the Impossible
Sarah (Part 1)
Life Application

Through decades of obedience to Jehovah and following God wherever He led, Sarah and her husband, Abraham, remained childless. Year after year, they watched other people have children and grandchildren. As Abraham and Sarah grew older, their chances to conceive grew smaller—and their hopes grew dimmer.

Then God appeared to Abraham and promised them offspring as numerous as the stars in the sky. Then many long years went by, and still, they had no baby.

Did they fight about it? Did Sarah accuse Abraham of mishearing God or of simply being crazy? Did they both wonder if God had tricked or lied to them? They must have questioned His timing, at least. At one point, Sarah even gave her maidservant, Hagar, to Abraham in an effort to help God's plan along.

But God had His own plan, and His timing couldn't be rushed. The scripture says that Sarah bore a son at exactly the right time.

This once-barren woman became a brand-new mom at a very old age. And her spouse, no spring chicken himself, found himself a father for the first time by Sarah. Maybe God waited so long to prove to them and to us that He alone is the author of life. Just when all hope was lost, God stepped in and did the impossible.

What in your life seems too hard for God? Is it your marriage, your children's behavior, or your financial status? All of the above?

Sometimes we pray about the things that consume our thoughts and no one seems to be listening. We view the situation with earthly, not heavenly eyes and think, *This situation is impossible!*

And many times, when God does answer, He takes much, much longer than we'd like. We get discouraged and feel like He's not concerned about us. Sometimes we even try to help the situation along—and often end up making it worse.

But God has His plan, and His timing can't be rushed. Whether we can feel Him or not, He's right in the thick of life with us. He longs to take our most precious hopes and dreams—even those secret longings and prayers you've told no one about—and fulfill them in surprising ways. Nothing—not sibling rivalry, a tumultuous marriage, or precarious finances—is too hard for Him.

Psalm 37:4 NIV says, "Delight yourself in the Lord and he will give you the desires of your heart." He longs to give us what will make us most happy—even if that means changing our desires to align more fully with His.

So Mom, don't lose hope. Your answer may be just around the corner, because your Father in heaven loves you, and He longs to see you smile. One day, you will be saying, "God has done the impossible," just like Sarah.

Think It Over

- What situation is a challenge to your faith?

- How have you dealt with it?

- What do you think the psalmist meant in Psalm 37:4?

- How does the story of Sarah inspire and encourage you?

> *Wait for the LORD; be strong and*
> *take heart and wait for the LORD.*
> PSALM 27:14 NIV

God Gave Laughter
Sarah (Part 2)
Abridged from Genesis 18 NLV

The Lord showed Himself to Abraham by the oak trees of Mamre, as he sat at the tent door in the heat of the day. Abraham looked up and saw three men standing in front of him. When he saw them, he ran from the tent door to meet them.

He put his face to the ground and said, "My lord, if I have found favor in your eyes, please do not pass by your servant. Let us have a little water brought to wash your feet. Rest yourselves under the tree. And I will get a piece of bread so you may eat and get strength. After that you may go on your way, since you have come to your servant."

The men said, "Do as you have said."

So Abraham ran into the tent to Sarah, and said, "Hurry and get three pails of fine flour, mix it well, and make bread."

Then Abraham ran to the cattle and took out a young and good calf. He gave it to the servant to make it ready in a hurry. He took milk and cheese and the meat which he had made ready, and set it in front of them. He stood by them under the tree while they ate.

Then they said to him, "Where is your wife Sarah?"

And he said, "There in the tent."

The Lord said, "I will be sure to return to you at this time next year. And your wife Sarah will have a son." Sarah was listening at the tent door behind him. Now Abraham and Sarah were old. . . . So Sarah laughed to herself, saying, "Will I have this joy after my husband and I have grown old?". . .

Then the men got up from there and looked down toward Sodom. Abraham went with them to send them on their way.

And the Lord said, "Should I hide from Abraham what I am about to do, since Abraham will become a great and powerful nation, because good will come to all the nations of the earth through him? For I have chosen him, so that he may teach his children and the sons of his house after him to keep the way of the Lord by doing what is right and fair, so the Lord may bring to Abraham what He has promised him."

God Gave Laughter
Sarah (Part 2)
Life Application

When she overheard the men telling her husband that God would give them a baby, Sarah, who had left hope behind long ago, laughed. *Me?* She thought. *Bear a child?*

The men didn't hear Sarah's laugh, but God did. "Why did Sarah laugh?" He wondered. "Is anything too hard for the Lord?"

Sarah denied chortling, but she was caught. *Maybe,* she must've thought, *God will keep His promise.* A little seed of hope grew in her heart.

As the seed grew, so did her belly. And her incredulity turned to hilarity of the best kind when she bore a son, just as God had promised. Abraham and Sarah named the boy Isaac, which means "laughter."

This grateful mom had known laughter of the worst kind, because to be barren in her society was to suffer ridicule and persecution. And now she knew the best kind of mirth—the kind that bubbles up from a heart bursting with fulfilled promises.

Sarah also learned to laugh at herself. As a new mom at ninety-plus, she needed a great sense of humor. There was no Starbucks in sight back then. She didn't even have *Parenting* magazine, binkies, or chocolate!

God wanted to give something more than a baby to Sarah. He desired to work in Sarah's heart, and she allowed Him to. And when her son came in fulfillment of God's promise, she hooted and hollered and gave the glory to her Maker.

Moms, we need to laugh more. Researchers have studied the effects of laughter on the immune system and concluded that laughing lowers blood pressure, reduces stress hormones, increases muscle flexion, and boosts immune function. Laughter also triggers the release of endorphins, the body's natural painkillers, and produces a general sense of well-being.

And for those of you who hate exercise, scientists have found that a belly laugh is equivalent to "internal jogging." Laughter can provide good cardiac conditioning. And frequent belly laughter empties your lungs of more air than laughing takes—similar to deep breathing.

Thankfully, we have a leg up on the rest of the world in this arena, because children are one of God's natural antidepressants. They laugh naturally and with abandon.

As moms, we have great laugh-inducers within arm's reach: our children. And kids don't just help us to laugh—they allow us to see ourselves differently. What mom doesn't melt when her three-year-old says, "You look pretty, Mommy"? And who could continue to take herself seriously after a child makes an honest, guileless—and yes, extremely embarrassing—comment in public?

So enjoy your children, and laugh out loud at their antics today. Hoot and holler, and give the glory to God. Who knows—you might just get a good workout!

Think It Over

• What kinds of things has God given you when you expected something else?

• What can you learn from Sarah?

• What makes you laugh?

• What was it that triggered your last good belly laugh?

> *A cheerful heart is good medicine,*
> *but a crushed spirit dries up the bones.*
> PROVERBS 17:22 NIV

Dreams for Our Children
Salome, Mother of James and John
Matthew 20:20–28 NLV

The mother of Zebedee's children (James and John) came to Jesus with her sons. She got down on her knees before Jesus to ask something of Him.

He said to her, "What do you want?"

She said, "Say that my two sons may sit, one at Your right side and one at Your left side, when You are King."

Jesus said to her, "You do not know what you are asking. Are you able to take the suffering that I am about to take? (Are you able to be baptized with the baptism that I am baptized with?)"

They said, "Yes, we are able."

He said to them, "You will suffer as I will suffer. But the places at My right side and at My left side are not Mine to give. Whoever My Father says will have those places."

The other ten followers heard this. They were angry with the two brothers.

Jesus called them to Him and said, "You know how the kings of the nations show their power to the people. Important leaders use their power over the people. It must not be that way with you. But whoever wants to be great among you, let him care for you. Whoever wants to be first among you, let him be your servant. For the Son of Man came not to be cared for. He came to care for others. He came to give His life so that many could be bought by His blood and made free from the punishment of sin."

Dreams for Our Children
Salome, Mother of James and John
Life Application

Picture an early-Christian version of a stage mom, and you've pegged Salome, the mother of James and John.

As mother to two of Jesus' disciples and the wife of a Jewish fisherman, she sought an opportunity for a better life. Can you blame her? After all, those who surrounded Jesus as He performed miracles and promised a new kingdom had been persecuted by their oppressors for what seemed like forever. So instead of hearing Jesus' words as promises of spiritual wealth and eternal life—they heard what they wanted to hear.

As Salome heard Jesus criticize the rulers of His day, she thought: *He's going to overthrow the Romans and give us all seats at the ruling table. Maybe someone will serve us for once!*

Sidling up to the Master, she said, "Lord, promise my sons that they'll sit on Your right and left!"

Jesus' stern rebuke embarrassed and quieted her. How long after that did she "get" what Jesus was about? Salome stood at a distance from the cross, along with Mary Magdalene and Mary, the mother of James. She watched as soldiers mocked her boys' hero, the man who called them and changed them. Later, she bought spices with the other faithful women to anoint Jesus' body.

Was she full of sorrow for Jesus—or for her boys' future? Hopefully, by the time of Jesus' crucifixion, she understood what He was trying to do and realized that His kingdom was not an earthly one.

When we pray for our own family's future, our goal should be God's glory—not selfish ambition. How simple, yet difficult, that is! So many times, we confuse what *we* want for our children with what God may want for them. We long for God to put his stamp of approval on our dreams for our family, instead of asking Him what our dreams should be.

Maybe we think about our kids' future career and see stars—literally. We believe they're unusually talented or beautiful, and start seeing dollar signs. And it's no wonder. After all, the society we live in rewards fame and talent much more so than character and integrity. It's easy to get caught up in that mentality and forget that God's plan for our children might not be the same as ours.

God might let our children fail (gasp!) or just be average. He desires their faithfulness (and ours)—not fame and fortune. Those things aren't wrong in themselves—but they can become idols.

Try to ask yourself, "Is God letting me/them lose or fail in order to grow?" and "Are my desires in line with His?"

The bottom line is: Do we just want to be happy with ourselves, or do we want to make God smile, too? When we answer this question honestly, it could change our perspective—and our lives.

Think It Over

- What kind of dreams do you have for your children?

- Pray about these dreams, and ask God whether or not they're appropriate.

- When has God let you fail?

- What do you think He was trying to teach you through that experience?

Look at that man, bloated by self-importance— full of himself but soul-empty. But the person in right standing before God through loyal and steady believing is fully alive, really alive.
HABAKKUK 2:4 MSG

Willing to Sacrifice
The Prostitute before Solomon
1 Kings 3:16–28 NLV

Then two women who sold the use of their bodies came to the king and stood in front of him. One of the women said, "O my lord, this woman and I live in the same house. And I gave birth to a child while she was in the house. On the third day after I gave birth, this woman gave birth to a child also. And we were alone. There was no one else with us in the house. There were only the two of us. This woman's son died during the night, because she lay on him. So she got up in the night and took my son from my side while I was asleep. She laid him in her arms, and her dead son in my arms. When I got up in the morning to nurse my son, I saw that he was dead. But when I came nearer and looked, I saw that he was not my son who was born to me."

Then the other woman said, "No! The living one is my son, and the dead one is your son."

But the first woman said, "No! The dead one is your son and the living one is my son." They spoke this way in front of the king.

Then the king said, "The one says, 'This is my son who is living, and your son is the dead one.' The other says, 'No! Your son is the dead one. My son is the living one.' " And the king said, "Bring me a sword." So they brought a sword to the king.

And the king said, "Divide the living child in two. Give half to the one woman and half to the other."

Then the mother of the living child had much pity

for her son and said to the king, "O, my lord, give her the living child. Do not kill him."

But the other woman said, "He will not be mine or yours. Divide him."

Then the king answered and said, "Give the first woman the living child. Do not kill him. She is his mother."

When all Israel heard how the king had decided, they were afraid of him. For they saw that the wisdom of God was in him, to do what is right and fair.

Willing to Sacrifice
The Prostitute in Solomon's Court
Life Application

The prostitute in King Solomon's court had a checkered past, but she knew she was a good mom. Perhaps her mother hadn't been there for her, and so she vowed to be the best parent possible from the moment she felt a stirring in her womb. She loved her child more than her own life, and she would do anything for her baby.

When the other woman standing before Solomon demanded that the child be given to her, the baby's real mom began to weep. And when Solomon threatened to cut the infant in half in order to please both women, she fell on the floor, inconsolable. "No, my lord!" she sobbed. "Please, let her take the baby. Don't harm my child, I beg you!"

King Solomon stood up, his height intimidating. The prostitute cowered in his presence, but her resolve was firm. She might never see her child again, but she would know that her baby was alive.

Then the King said, "Give the baby to this woman," and he pointed at her. "She's the real mother."

"Oh, my King, thank you," the prostitute choked out, as she stood and reached out for her child. "Thank you so much!" She whispered a prayer of thanks, one she would utter over and over in the next few days. Her precious child was safe in her arms again. The baby looked deep into the mother's eyes, and joy welled up in her heart.

Moms have to be prepared to give up their time, money, and dreams for the sake of their children. Some mothers—especially single parents—have to be willing to give up practically everything in order to see their children thrive.

Such is also the life of those with special-needs children. Moms with disabled or sick kids sacrifice all their resources to help their children have a normal life.

One mom with a chronically ill child spends hundreds of hours every month in her car, driving back and forth to the hospital. She and her husband cut every luxury out of their budget to afford gas, doctor bills, and time off from work.

Another mom with an autistic child works a nightshift so she can be with her child during the day, since she's divorced and can't afford therapy on her monthly child support. She's forgotten what a social life is, and she can't remember the last time she had time by herself.

These moms are heroes, willing to give up their own agendas and desires to give their kids whatever they need. And they do it without a lot of fanfare. They do it because they're moms, and they know it's just what they're supposed to do.

Next time you see a mom like this, tell her that you're praying for her. Better yet, follow through and say that prayer, asking God to comfort, encourage, and strengthen her in her Herculean struggles.

Think It Over

- What have you given up to be a good mom?

- What are you afraid of giving up? List those things and pray about them.

- How can you encourage a worn-out mom of a special-needs child?

And don't forget to do good and to share with those in need. These are the sacrifices that please God.
HEBREWS 13:16 NLT

A Miracle of Provision
The Widow of Zarephath
Abridged from 1 Kings 17 NLV

Then the word of the Lord came to him, saying, "Get up and go to Zarephath. . .and stay there. I have told a woman there, whose husband has died, to feed you." So Elijah got up and went to Zarephath.

When he came to the city gate, he saw a woman there gathering sticks. He called to her and said, "I ask of you, get me a little water in a jar, that I may drink."

As she was going to get it, he called to her, "I ask of you, bring me a piece of bread in your hand."

But she said, "As the Lord your God lives, I have no bread. I only have enough flour in the jar to fill a hand, and a little oil in the jar. See, I am gathering a few sticks so I may go in and make it ready for me and my son. Then we will eat it and die."

Elijah said to her, "Have no fear. Go and do as you have said. But make me a little loaf of bread from it first, and bring it out to me. Then you may make one for yourself and for your son. For the Lord God of Israel says, 'The jar of flour will not be used up. And the jar of oil will not be empty, until the day the Lord sends rain upon the earth.'"

So she went and did what Elijah said. And she and he and those of her house ate for many days. The jar of flour was not used up, and the jar of oil did not become empty. It happened as was spoken by the word of the Lord through Elijah.

After this the son of the woman who owned the

house became sick. His sickness was so bad that there was no breath left in him.

So the woman said to Elijah, "What do I have to do with you, O man of God? You have come to me to have my sin be remembered, and to kill my son!"

He said to her, "Give me your son." Then he took him from her arms and carried him up to the room on the second floor where he stayed. And he laid him on his own bed. He called to the Lord and said, "O Lord my God, have You brought trouble to the woman I am staying with, by making her son die?"

Then he lay upon the child three times and called to the Lord, saying, "O Lord my God, I pray to You. Let this child's life return to him." The Lord heard the voice of Elijah. And the life of the child returned to him and he became strong again.

Elijah took the child and brought him down from the second floor into the house and gave him to his mother. He said, "See, your son is alive."

Then the woman said to Elijah, "Now I know that you are a man of God. Now I know that the word of the Lord in your mouth is truth."

A Miracle of Provision
The Widow of Zarephath
Life Application

In Elijah's day, a widow had few resources. As a woman, she needed a man to take care of her—not the other way around. Yet God sent Elijah to the widow at Zarephath so she could provide for him. Why? So he, in turn, could giver her what she needed—not just physically, but also spiritually.

First, she needed food. Like Old Mother Hubbard, her cupboard was bare. She only had a little bit of flour and some oil. And judging by her response to the man of God, the widow and her son had not eaten much for quite some time. But when she obeyed Elijah's instructions, God performed a miracle. The bin of flour and jar of oil was replenished, day after day.

Still, the woman had trouble accepting that God had sent Elijah—or that God even existed. She had seen enough hardship and trouble to make her doubt God's faithfulness. And when her son became ill and died, the tragedy seemed to confirm her worst fears. *God isn't good*, she thought. *Maybe He's doing this to punish me.* Grief-stricken, she railed at Elijah and at her Maker.

Elijah had obviously grown close to the widow by this time, and with compassion, he grabbed her dead son, carried the boy to his room, and pleaded with God to resurrect him.

When God heard Elijah's cry, He brought the boy back to life. And in so doing, He provided nourishment for the widow's soul.

Another widow, Connie, looked in her pantry and sighed. She worked two jobs to keep the bills paid, but the groceries just didn't seem to last as long as they used to. She didn't know how she was going to stretch her meager supply of food until payday.

Fighting back tears, Connie prayed. *Lord, it's me again. I know You know my situation, and You've helped me so many times before. Please give me some ideas, and if it's not too much trouble, could You even do a miracle?*

In answer to her prayer, Connie remembered that her kids loved a simple casserole that she hadn't fixed in a while. *Do I have all the ingredients?* she wondered. She found most of them. *If only I had one can of cream of mushroom soup, I could fix this meal,* she thought.

Suddenly, the doorbell rang. *Who can that be?* Connie wondered as she went to the door. Opening it, she saw her neighbor, an elderly lady. "Sue!" Connie exclaimed. "How are you?"

"Good, sweetie," Sue said, "but I have this can of soup Millard and I can't use anymore. We just got back from the doctor and he told us no more salt. I wondered if your kids would eat it in something."

Sure enough, when Connie looked at the can, it was cream of mushroom soup. Awed at God's timing and faithfulness, she tearfully accepted the gift from her neighbor.

God can always be trusted to provide for His children, just like He did for the widow of Zarephath. If you're weary and worried, rest in that fact today.

Think It Over

- How has God provided for you in a miraculous way?

- What worries do you have? Journal about them today.

- Pray over your worries one by one, entrusting them to God.

"So don't worry about these things, saying, 'What will we eat? What will we drink? What will we wear?' These things dominate the thoughts of unbelievers, but your heavenly Father already knows all your needs. Seek the Kingdom of God above all else, and live righteously, and he will give you everything you need."
MATTHEW 6:31–33 NLT

Conclusion

Mom, what's your need today? Do you long to get a handle on your finances? Are the children driving you crazy? Are you tired, burned out, and ready for a break?

The moms we've visited in these devotionals knew just how you're feeling. They dealt with circumstances we can't even imagine, as well as some that we find common. They faced many trials and challenges, but God always saw them through.

He gave Rachel, Hannah, and Sarah children and the joys of seeing their broods grow. He supported Eunice as she raised Timothy to follow the Lord. He granted Eve joys, too, though they were laced with sorrow. Naomi found hope through the gift of Ruth. Jochebed found comfort in nursing the baby she gave up. Hagar found God in the desert and realized that He saw her. Leah found the strength to endure being unloved. And Job's wife saw her husband's decimated fortunes increase to twice what he'd had before.

Whatever you long for, know that God is the One who made you, who delights in you, and who will give you what you need. Scripture is clear—those who trust in Him will not be disappointed. They will find their deepest desires fulfilled and their hearts changed.

Hold onto that promise as the chaos of motherhood swirls around you. And, above all else, hold onto His Word.

When you do, you'll be amazed at what happens.